Computer Programming for Beginners

The essential guide on Python with hand-on projects. Coding for beginners. Consecutive steps from the basic to the advanced level

Tim Wired

Table of Contents

Learn Python

Python Data Science

Coding with Python

Learn Python

Crash Course to Learn Algorithms Just By Doing Some Practice. It Will Really Help Your Career Out

TIM WIRED

Introduction

Congratulations on purchasing *Learn Python* and thank you for doing so.

We are going to spend some time taking a look at how to work not only with the Python language, and how we are able to use this to handle some of our machine learning and the different algorithms that we are able to do with this if your business is going to handle some of the work with data science as well. There are a lot of options and benefits of working with this data science, and handling this whole process is going to be difficult in some situations as well. This guidebook is going to spend some time working with data science, and how Python is going to work to help us get the algorithms done and seeing the patterns and insights that are found inside of that data as well.

There are a lot of different parts that happen with data science and Python that we are to handle when it comes to our business. We will start out with a simple look at the Python language, how to work with the benefits of Python, and so much more.

After we will look at some of the work that we are able to do with machine learning. Machine learning is going to be some of the backbones that we are able to look at when it is time to handle all of the different data that we are able to work with to improve our business. Understanding how this works, and how it can combine with Python in order to work with the algorithms will be discussed later in this guidebook as well. Along with learning some of the information that we need about machine learning, we will also take a look at some of the different ways that we can work with machine learning and more.

Then we get to some of the meat and potatoes that we are able to see when it comes to working with machine learning and Python. There are so many great algorithms that you are able to focus on when it is time to work with the data that you have, and it really depends on what kind of data you are working with, what information you would like to find out of all that, and what we hope to accomplish out of all this as well.

This guidebook will go more into some of the algorithms that you are able to work with along the way as well. We will look at how to handle the decision trees and random forests, neural networks, support vector machines, clustering, KNN, and so much more. This is going to help us to really understand how to work with machine learning and how to pick out the right option that we are able to work with when it is time to start with our own algorithms as well.

There is so much that we are able to work with the Python language, especially when we want to work with machine learning and creating some of the algorithms and more that we would like to handle. If you have been looking at data science and hoping to make it work for some of the things that you want to do like understanding your customer, learning more about the industry, and beating your competition, you will find that this is going to be one of the best methods to help you to get more out of the process as well. When you are ready to get started with the process of data science and machine learning from Python, make sure to check out this guidebook to help you get started.

There are plenty of books on this subject on the market, thanks again for choosing this one! Every effort was made to ensure it is full of as much useful information as possible, please enjoy it!

Chapter 1: What is the Python Language?

Before we get a chance to go more into machine learning and all that this cool technology is able to do for us, we first need to take a closer look at some of the coding that is going to happen behind the scenes with this language. There are so many algorithms and other parts of the process that go on behind the scenes here that it is important for us to take some time to learn about them. This is so we can get a more accurate view of what is happening in Python.

The language that we are going to focus on when it is time to handle machine learning is the Python language. There may be a lot of different options that we are able to focus on when we want to do some machine learning. You will find that the Python language is going to be one of the best options to work with. There are a ton of benefits that come with the Python language, and that is one of the main reasons why we will want to choose this option over some of the others.

This chapter is going to spend some time taking a look at the benefits of Python and all of the reasons why it is going to provide us with some of the results that we want when it comes to machine learning and some of the algorithms that we want to focus on here. Python is one of the best options that we are able to use to get this done because of all the great features, and as we go through this guidebook, we will see more about how we are able to use this for our needs.

You are more than likely excited to get into some of the work that can happen with machine learning and some of the algorithms that we will talk about in a bit. But before we are able to get to that point and start using this for our needs, we need to learn more about the Python language. Some of the different parts of the Python language that we need to learn and explore before combining it together with machine learning and data science includes:

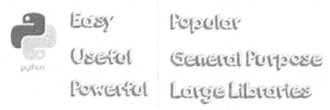

Python Programming Language

Easy   Popular

Useful   General Purpose

Powerful   Large Libraries

How to Work with the Python Language

If you are interested in working with Python, there are going to be a few basic concepts that we need to focus on ahead of time to make sure that we are able to use this language in the manner that we would like. First, we have to understand that Python is a language that does not need to rely on compiling to get the results that it needs. Python is going to be a language that is interpreted. This means that you are able to run the program as soon as you make some changes to the file. This is a nice thing because it is going to make things like iterating, revising, and troubleshooting the program much faster than what you will see with some of the other languages out there.

As you will quickly see when you work with the Python language, this is actually one of the easier ones to code in. Even as someone who has not spent a lot of time working with Python, and you haven't been able to do any coding in the past, you will find that it is easy enough to learn, and you can easily have a basic program up and running and ready to go in just a few minutes when working on this option.

As you get onto the Python language, assuming that you already have it downloaded and installed on your computer, it is a good idea to spend some time messing around and learning about the interpreter. You are able to use this interpreter from Python to test out some of the code that you have, without having to add it to the program to do this. This is going to be one of the best ways for a beginner to learn more about how a specific command is going to work, or it can allow you to write away a program that you would like to just practice with before throwing out.

We can also work with this in order to learn a bit about how Python is able to handle some of the variables and objects that are found in your codes. Python is unique in that it is considered one of the object-oriented languages, or OOP. This means that all of the parts that show up in the program are going to be treated as objects.

Along the same line, you will not need to go through and declare the variables that you are doing at the beginning of the program because you are able to do this at any time that is the easiest for your coding instead. This one also doesn't require that you go through and specify the type of variable that you are using, so it will not matter if you are working with a string, integer, or not, because the compiler will be able to figure this all out for you.

These are just a few of the parts that we need to know more about when it comes to handling the Python language. This is a really great language to work with, and it comes with a ton of intricate parts that have to work together in a strong manner in order to see some of the success that we would like. When we are able to put all of these parts together and learn how to make them work, you will find that it is easier than ever to really write out some of the codes that we want, even within the Python language.

The Benefits of Python

When it comes to picking out a coding language, you will find that there are a lot of benefits that will come from using Python, and many reasons why you are able to use this coding language rather than some of the others that are out there. This language is simple to learn and perfect for someone who is just getting started with coding, to make sure that they are able to get their coding done in the manner that they would like.

In fact, the Python language has been designed in order to make it easier for some of the coding that we want to do, even as a beginner. It is written out in the English language, and some of the codes that come with it are simple enough to make life a little bit easier. Even if you have never gone through and done any coding at all, you will find that this language is going to be easier to handle even for you as a beginner.

Even though this is going to be a coding language that is meant to help us as a beginner, it still has some of the power that you need in order to get the coding done. Even when it comes to machine learning and some of the harder parts that we need with the different algorithms that show up throughout this guidebook, you will find that we are able to use Python to get it all done. There are some of those who are going to be worried about Python being too easy for them to work with some of the more complex things that they want to have along the way, but as we take a look at how this language actually works and what we are able to do with it, you will find that it is able to handle any of the different things that you would like along the way, no matter how simple or complex they may be.

This is just the start of the benefits that we are able to see when it comes to working with the Python language. There are quite a few benefits that we are able to focus on as well, and these are going to include options like:

1. A large community that we are able to work with and enjoy. One thing that a lot of people who are starting out with machine learning are going to really like about this process is that there is such a large community that they are able to work with. This helps them to find the right answers when they have questions or concerns, or when there is something that is just not working out for them. This community is going to include a lot of programmers of all different types of degrees of knowledge including those who have been coding for a long time, those who are newer, and some that are in between. This is a great resource for you to use to get the results that you want in the process.

2. Lots of libraries and extensions that you are able to utilize. As you get into some of the work that you want to do with the Python language, you will find that it is going to be a great option to help you to get your done with python overall. There are libraries to help you with machine learning, deep learning,

artificial intelligence, math, science, and so much more in the process.

3. I can work with machine learning. One of the biggest reasons that a lot of programmers like to· learn more about the Python language is because it is going to be able to work well with machine learning. Machine learning is a big thing for a lot of businesses as it helps them to reach their customers and basically sorts through large amounts of data for them in less time. Since Python can be used to handle and even run some of the algorithms that are critical to machine learning, we can see how the two go hand in hand, and why so many people and companies want to learn how to use this for their own needs as well.

4. It is considered an OOP language to make things easier: OOP languages, or object programming languages, are going to be those that can help us to keep the code organized with the help of classes and objects. We are able to create the classes that we want, and they work as boxes to hold onto the various objects that show up in our code as well. This is basically a method that we are able to use that keeps things organized and ensures that we are

able to take care of all the parts that we need in our code, without any of the headaches that may have been more prevalent in the older coding languages.

5. It can provide us with the options to combine together with some of the other languages that you need to get the job done. Sometimes, especially when we are working with some of the things that we want to get done in machine learning, we will find that we will need to work with another language other than Python to make it happen. The neat thing is that we are able to use some of the libraries that work well with Python, such as TensorFlow, to write out the codes that we want in Python, and then the library will go back and convert it into another language to execute it the way that we would like. It is that simple.

a. This is a great feature that we are able to enjoy when it comes to working with Python and getting it to do some of the work that we would like along the way. You can combine some of the ease of use of Python with some of the other languages out there and find that it provides you all of the benefits that you are looking for.

There are a lot of different options that we are able to work with when it comes to the Python language. This language has a lot that we are able to use when it comes to creating this kind of program and will really help us to see some of the results that we need when it comes to handling all of our coding needs. There may be other coding languages that we are able to work with, but none of them are going to provide us with the power, versatility, and ease of use that we are able to get with Python. And with that in mind, we are going to spend some time through this guidebook looking at what Python is all about, and how we are able to use it to help us get some of our work done in machine learning as well.

Chapter 2: Understanding the World of Machine Learning

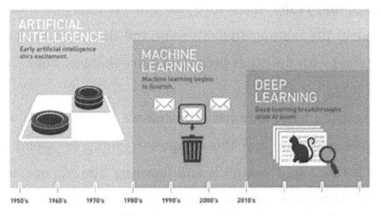

Now that we know a little bit more about the Python language and all of the things that we are able to do with that language to make our work easier to handle, it is time for us to enter into the world of machine learning as well. There are a lot of different parts that come with machine learning, and it is going to help our business to gain a good advantage and get ahead of the competition as well. To keep it simple for now though (we will take a look at some of the algorithms that we are able to use with this one later on), we are going to focus our attention on understanding the world of machine learning and how it is going to work to train our systems and our computers.

To start, machine learning is basically going to be a process that helps us, through the use of a variety of algorithms, to properly train some of our systems to make decisions on their own. With the right algorithms in place, we are able to go through and really make sure that our systems and more will behave in the manner that we want and that they will be able to interact with the other people who use them as well.

This is just a basic summary of what we are going to see with machine learning, and this chapter is going to spend some more time going through it and learning how we are able to make this work for some of our needs as well. Some of the different parts of machine learning that we need to take some time to explore now will include:

What is Machine Learning?

The first thing that we need to take a look at is the basics of machine learning. To keep it simple, we will find that machine learning is going to be the application of artificial intelligence that is going to offer our machines and systems the ability to learn and act in a manner that is similar to humans, without us having to program them on our own. This process of learning is something that can get better and improve over time and is going to happen when we feed new information and data into the machine, and even when the system gets to have interactions and observations with the real-world through use of that particular program run by machine learning.

When we are working with a system of machine learning, there are going to be three main components that we need to spend some of our time on. These will include the model, parameters, and also the learner. Let's start at the beginning of the model. This model is going to be the system that is in place that can help us to make predictions or identifications. If we have the right model in place, it is easier to go through all of that information and really find the insights and predictions that we need.

From there, we are able to focus on some of the parameters that are found in a machine learning system. These are unique because they are going to be any of the signals or factors that the model is going to use in order to form the decisions that it makes. And then there is a learner, which is going to be any of the systems that will be able to adjust the model, usually by making some adjustments to the parameters by observing the differences in the predictions versus the actual outcome that we want.

The working of any machine learning system is going, to begin with, to help the model. In the beginning, you will need to give the model a prediction to the system. The model is going to depend on these parameters being in place before it is able to make any of the calculations that we need. The system of machine learning is then going to be able to use its own mathematical equation to help express the parameters and to efficiently form a trend line of what it should actually do.

So, the real-life information is going to be entered as soon as that model is set. For the most part, the real score is not going to match up with the model. Some of these are going to be above, and sometimes, we will see some show up below the predicted line that is there. And this is where some of the learning components that we want to see with machine learning is going to get started.

This information that we are able to provide to the system of machine learning is going to be known as our training data. This training data is important because the learner can utilize it to train itself so that the model learns how to behave and gets better at the work that it is doing. The learner is then going to observe the scores and determine the difference between what the model is getting and the actual results that it should get. Then it is able to use some math in order to adjust some of the assumptions that were initially made. Now, with the new set of scores and some of the adjustments that were run along the way, we will be able to run through the system again.

After this, the comparison is going to happen and will be completed between the revised model that the learner just came up with, and the real score as well. If it is successful, the scores are going to be at least a little bit closer to the prediction in this option than they were in the first place. However, this doesn't mean that they are going to be ideal. We do need to go through this process a few times in order to help make sure that the system gets as accurate as possible.

So, after this second round, the parameters will need to be adjusted again so that the learner is able to reshape their model again. You will have to work through the comparisons over and over again until the model is able to predict the outcome in an accurate manner.

This system of machine learning is going to make adjustments again and again in this kind of manner, at least until things get right. This is going to be something that is known as gradient learning or gradient descent. And while this is a process that can take some time and may not be as easy to work with as we might hope, you will find that it is a good way to take a look at how this kind of system is able to learn and get better at the job that it should do.

What Can Machine Learning Be Used For?

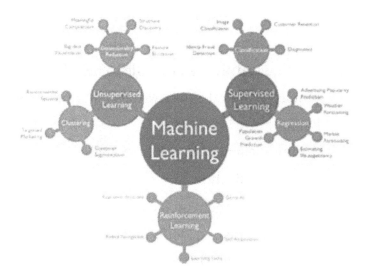

The next thing that we are able to take a look at here is some of the ways that we are able to use machine learning for some of our needs. Machine learning is going to be usable in a lot of different sectors, and the uses of this kind of language are likely to grow over time, as we develop new and exciting ways that we can work with it as well. Some of the sectors that are able to work with machine learning will include:

1. We will find that machine learning is going to have a lot of applications that we are able to enjoy whether we are working with the healthcare world, retail, publishing, and so many other industries.

2. Google and Facebook are going to work with machine learning in order to help push the relevant kind of advertisements based on the behaviors of the searching for that user in the past.

3. Machine learning is also able to handle some multi-dimensional and multi-variety data inside of some dynamic environment.

4. Machine learning is going to enable us to have the efficient utilization and time cycle reduction of all the resources that you have.

5. When we take a look at data entry, machine learning is able to help us simplify some of the documentation that tends to take a lot of time in the first place.

6. Machine learning is going to help us to improve some of the precision that we are going to see in the models and rules in the world of finances.

7. Machine learning is also going to help detect spam in emails and messages.

8. Machine learning is going to allow us to have an appropriate lifetime value prediction and can make it easier for us to segment the customers better than before.

9. Machine learning is going to assist when it comes to accurately forecasting sales and can make marketing for our products so much easier overall.

Machine Learning vs. Artificial Intelligence

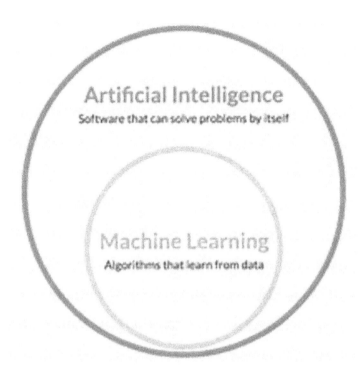

Another thing that we need to get started with is how machine learning and artificial intelligence are going to work. Both of these are going to be used interchangeably in many cases, especially when it comes to big data. But we have to learn that these are not going to be the same things, and we need to be able to see some of the differences that come with them.

To start with, artificial intelligence is going to be a branch that is found inside of computer science and can be defined as the ability of a machine or a computer program to help learn from experience and will perform tasks in the same way as humans. We can now take a look at the differences between machine learning and artificial intelligence in the information that is below.

First, we can take a closer look at artificial intelligence. This is going to be a broader concept that is going to address the use of machines to perform the tasks that are considered smart. The goal here is to enhance the chances of success, but it does not ensure that there is accuracy. In addition, AI is going to be a higher cognitive process, and it is going to function more like a computer program that is going to perform smart work. This helps to lead to wisdom or intelligence. In addition, we are going to see that it involves the creation of a system that is able to mimic the behavior of humans.

Then we are able to take a look at machine learning. This is going to be one of the applications of artificial intelligence, and it is going to be based on the idea of giving machine access to data that it needs and allowing them to learn for themselves. The goal is to enhance the accuracy, but it doesn't care about success. Machine learning enables the system to learn from the data.

Another thing to look at is that machine learning is going to be a simple concept where a machine is able to take the data and then learn from it. Machine learning is always a good thing because it is going to lead to more knowledge. Machine learning is then going to lead to the creation of algorithms that are self-learning.

The Different Types of Machine Learning

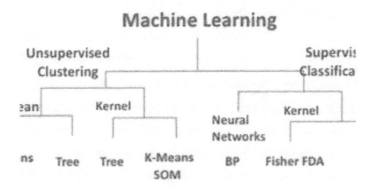

To help us to break down some of the real problems that we have with this work, and to make sure that we have a machine learning system that is able to tackle it all, we need to get to know more about the algorithms types that come with machine learning. There are our main types of algorithms that we are able to work with, and often it depends on the kind of work that we want to do with them to help us choose which one to pick. The four main types of learning algorithms that we are able to work with are going to include:

1. Supervised

2. Unsupervised

3. Semi-supervised

4. Reinforcement

First, we are able to take a look at the kind that is known as supervised machine learning. These are going to be the ones that will contain a target or an outcome variable, and sometimes a dependent variable, which is going to be predicted from the set of independent variables that we give to it. A function that is able to map out the inputs to the desired outputs can be generated while doing these variables as well.

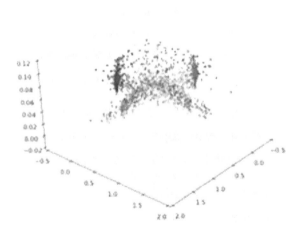

Basically, these kinds of algorithms are going to take a lot of examples that they can hold onto and will learn from those.

We need to make sure that we have a lot of labeled data to make this work though. The algorithm is able to take the information that it is provided, look over the input and the corresponding output, and then figure out how to use this new knowledge to their advantage in order to make good predictions about new data that the algorithm sees in the future.

The second type of learning algorithm that we are able to work with is going to be the unsupervised machine learning. This is the one that we are going to work with when we don't have an outcome of some kind of target variable for helping us to estimate or make some of the predictions that you need. So, you will find that with this one we are not going to tell the system where we would like it to go.

Instead, our system is going to need to learn how to understand where to go and what answers to give from the data that we provide to it in the first place. This is going to happen when the algorithms are able to utilize techniques that will input data to detect patterns, groups, and summarize the points of data, mine for rules, and even describe the data to those who want to use it in a manner that is much better than before.

The algorithms that come with this one are going to be used mainly to help out with pattern detection and descriptive modeling. These algorithms are going to be used in many cases where human experts are not going to know what to look for in the data. There are a lot of algorithms that come with this will include the Apriori algorithm, K-means, and more.

The third option that we need to work with is going to be known as semi-supervised machine learning. In the other two types of algorithms, either the label is going to be there for the observations, or there are not going to be variables for all of the different observations that we want to use. This kind of learning is going to fall kind of in the middle of supervised and unsupervised learning that we talked about already. This is because it is going to rely on both labeled data and unlabeled data.

You will find that with the semi-supervised type of learning, accuracy is going to be improved quite a bit because we are able to use a small amount of data that is labeled along with some of the unlabeled data to help us train the work that we need to get done. There are quite a few options that you are able to use in order to help get this kind of learning done.

The final option that we are able to focus our attention on is going to be known as reinforcement machine learning. This is going to be the kind where we are not going to have any sets of data that are labeled or unlabeled, so it is not going to be like the other options that we talked about before. It is going to work in a way that will have the machine live in an environment of trial and error, and the machine is able to learn in this manner.

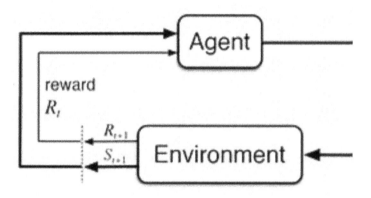

The machine that has some reinforcement algorithms working on it is going to be trained in order to make some business decisions that are accurate by learning from the experiences that it has had in the past, and then capturing the best knowledge that its possible knowledge. This kind of learning is going to be powerful but more complex than some of the other options, and it is going to help us to get a lot of cool things done with the work that we want to do as well.

There are so many ways that you are able to work with machine learning and ensure that it is going to do some of the work that you would like along the way. Learning more about how this can work and what we are able to do with it is going to make a world of difference in the way that we can handle some of the data science that we want to accomplish, and how we can make sure that the computer is going to learn in the manner that we would like.

Many businesses like to work with machine learning because they like all that this is able to do for them, and all of the benefits that they are able to get along the way as well. Machine learning can make it possible to learn from a lot of data that you have collected, in a manner that is faster and more efficient than what we are able to do manually. These predictions and insights can help us to make better decisions that propel our businesses forward and will ensure that we are going to see some of the best results for this in the process as well.

We will explore through this guidebook some of the many great things that you are able to do when it comes to working with machine learning, especially when you talk about how it works with the Python language. And we will look at some of the neat things that we are able to do when it is time to handle these algorithms, in all of the categories that we talked about before. This will help us to really learn more about how we can use machine learning to further our business.

Chapter 3: What are These Algorithms Used For?

As many products that work with machine learning start to grow and will continue to target enterprise throughout the world, you will find that these products are going to start to make a divergence into two channels. The first one is going to be the products that are going to become increasingly meta in order to make sure that machine learning itself is going to do better with its own predictive capacity. And then we are going to end up with those that are going to be more granular in their focus by addressing some of the specific problems that the verticals are going to experience sometimes.

And while the latest type of products in machine learning through both of these channels can reduce some of the points of pain in data science, especially for those that are used in a more business environment, there are some experts that warn that machine learning, no matter how much it grows, is not going to be able to solve two main issues, no matter the predictive capacity of these tools. These include:

1. Solving some of the unique problems for a particular business use case.

2. Cleaning up the data that you are using in the first place so that it is actually valuable in the workflow that is needed with machine learning.

A Look to Begin

When we first hear about machine learning and the term artificial intelligence, these are often going to be mistaken for some of the technologies that are out there that we think can replace people. Computers will find people, sell them the things that they want and need, and then there is no need any longer to have a human work in marketing, for example.

However, as more of this technology comes out, and it becomes a bigger part of or lives, it turns out that these technologies are still going to need some human interaction and help in order to get things done. They are not able to replace our jobs and the work that we are able to do, no matter how strong or powerful they may seem when we first get started.

Computers can do some of the grunge work there, but only humans are able to really take the information, see what matters the most, and then use it. Marketers and other fields are not going to be replaced with this automation and the user of machine learning, but they will find that using it can be in their best interest and can help them to complete their job in a more effective manner.

The first thing that we are able to look at here is how to take note of what machine learning is able to do, and where it is going to lack. You are able to program it in a manner to help seek out attributes and even count how many clicks we are going to be able to get on a particular website. This can be great news because it helps us to really learn from the data that we have for a long time to come.

Machine learning is even able to take this a bit further by recognizing the subject lines of a campaign. It can help us to tag images when we are doing a visual search, it can analyze the sentences that it sees, and undertake some decision-making in real-time, do power recommendation engines, and even engage in bidding that happens in the real world.

These are some of the amazing things that we are going to see when it comes to artificial intelligence or machine learning. Both of these are going to be best applied either when there is going to be a large surplus of the consumer or when you are in a business process that is more low yield than others. While there are a lot of functions that we are able to work with the help of machine learning, you will find that there are some places where it is going to be lacking as well. And we will be able to look through some of those in this chapter as well.

For example, we should not waste our time trying to apply machine learning and all that it is able to do to tasks where humans are already able to do them in an effective manner. This would be something like air traffic control when we are in an airport. If there is already a task that is pretty optimized overall, incorporating some machine learning into it would not really serve any purpose, and it would definitely not provide us with a good return on investment for our time either. By learning, we will find that AI, and the processes that come with machine learning, can become smarter in the process.

We have already seen that machine learning and artificial intelligence are found across the entirety of marketing and sales. And this is just one of the places that we are able to use this kind of technology. The more that we spend our time learning how to work through this, the more uses we are going to find with this kind of process as well.

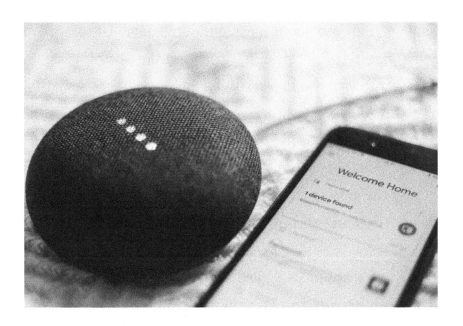

Avoiding Error

Before machine learning is as effective as we want, the machine has to be able to learn. Programmers are often going to shovel a lot of data, terabytes, or more into the hopper, all gladly digested by the learning algorithm that they chose. Ironically though, the system is no less human than those who are building it all up. This means that there will be some errors lurking if we are not careful and if we just throw all of the information together without spending time on it along the way. We need to make sure that we screen it out along the way as well.

We can take a look at an example of this with Lattice Engines. This is a solution that will look for patterns in the data in order to identify who is likely to convert to a sale. According to this company, they use about 8 percent of the data just to train the model that they are working with. Then the rest of it is going to be set aside to use in testing the model, which is something that we need to do with all of our products. This extra 20 percent is going to be used in order to test the model to see if it is able to make some accurate predictions. This is done because the answer is already known, and we can check to see how well this process is going to work along the way.

If machine learning is considered king in the industry, then data is going to be the queen in this relationship. If you don't have enough or rich training data, then no algorithm for machine learning is going to do the job, no matter how good it is. The best way to make sure that you are picking out data that is higher in quality and works for the programming that you are doing is to use more data. Often confidence in your data is going to come when we are able to get a different perspective on the same data but from different sources. If a lot of sources end up agreeing, then we know that the data is more likely to be true as well.

For many situations, the data, especially the analysis, and other solutions will be used by many companies right now. Data is going to be used in order to help out with the training, and then we are able to measure the validation, improve the model that we have, and understand the differences that we need to address as well. This also needs to have an extra layer to help us to remove some of the outliers. If we find that there is something that is not right with the data, then things are going to end up suffering from the algorithm that we are working with.

Remember here that quality is not going to be guaranteed all of the time, but quantity is something that can help us to make up for all of this. With data sets that are smaller, the impact of some of the bad data is going to be so much worse as well. Whenever we see that someone is failing, it is often because the set of data that they worked with was too small.

Keep the Programmers in the Loop

Another thing that we need to remember when we are working with this is that machine learning should not be something that we put on autopilot. Instead, it is going to be the co-pilot in the projects that we are working with. We need to have a person there who is able to make some good judgment calls on the output that the machine is able to provide to us.

Machine learning is able to do a lot of really cool things, but it is also still a relatively new technology, and there is still room to find some error. There are a few methods that we are able to use in order to put some constraints on the problem. All AI systems should take the feedback from humans or the overrides, and then can provide some justification for some of the actions. The transparency of the AI actions is going to be an absolute requirement for building up some trust with the users that we have.

Machine learning is able to do some of the programming tasks that we need that are not really possible for humans. For example, it is able to go through a year or more of data and see what is inside of it in just a few minutes. But then there are things that humans are able to do that may not seem possible for a machine. Does the pattern spotted by a machine seem to make sense for what is going on? Or does it end up being something more like an anomaly and doesn't make a lot of sense along the way? When there are a lot of variables to look at, we should allow the computer with machine learning to go through it all and figure out what is there. But we still need to be the second eyes or ears that are on it to see what is there.

While the machine is able to get some amazing results in a short amount of time, we have to remember that it is not always invincible in this process, and we need to make sure that it is going to work well. We are able to take a look at it with some fresh eyes, and then figure out whether it all makes sense or not. We have to be that second pair of eyes though, or this process is going to end up failing us along the way.

What Can Machine Learning Do?

Now that we have a bit more information on machine learning and how amazing it can be for some of our own success, it is time for us to dive in to some of the different things that we are able to do when we bring out the technology and some of the algorithms that come with machine learning. There are actually a lot of different things that we are able to use machine learning for overall if we just take the time to learn what they are and how we are able to benefit from them overall. Some of the different ways that companies are using machine learning, and how you may be using machine learning too without realizing it would include the following:

Helping us to detect spam in our email. Think about how tedious and boring it would be if you had to spend all of your tie sorting through emails and seeing which ones were spam and which ones were important. This would take forever, and we would probably give up on using email overall in the first place. This is where machine learning is going to come into play. Most of the major email providers that we use today, such as Gmail, will use techniques of machine learning in order to filter out spam emails.

This works because the algorithm that will run the email server will be trained on data first. The data it is trained on will include past emails that were spam so that it knows which phrases and words and even which email addresses are likely to be spam. Over time, it will even be able to get better at the job, and this can provide you with some powerful coding in the process. Sometimes, spam gets through, but it is a whole lot less than what you would get if this information we're able to just get through.

The next way that machine learning is able to help us out is with face recognition. With this kind of task, machines are able to identify someone just from a photo, and sometimes, from videos as the technology continues to progress as well. For example, we can use this to figure out who is authorized to go into a certain system, to get onto email, or just to recognize who is in a picture on Facebook, for example.

One of the methods of machine learning that you are likely to use on a regular basis is speech recognition. If you have used some of the popular assistants that are able to recognize your voice and respond to you, such as Alexa or your own phone for that matter, then you have seen one of the more popular applications of machine learning already at work.

There are a lot of devices that we use today that are going to rely on speech recognition in order to get things done. This can include options like Google Now and Amazon Echo just to name a few. The fundamental idea of these is that there can be interactions between the computer and the human through voice. And the more times that you use the device, the more it can learn your own individual speech patterns and what you are requesting, and the better it is at helping get things done.

The next option that we are able to see when it comes to how well machine learning can help us get things done is with the help of computer vision and image classification. We can see this when we take a look at Google Photos. This is a technology that is able to create some image filtering based on an object or a person we decide on.

Facebook is working with this as well. Their AI research lab is always looking for some new ways in order to improve the experiences of the user through things like image classification. The hope with this is to make it so that even those who are blind can have the AI describe the content that is in an image.

Many marketers are working with machine learning as well. This helps them to reach the right customers at the right times when they place their ads and makes it so that they are not wasting money along the way either. Some of the different advertisements that we are already seeing would be options like sponsored ads or Google Ad Sense. We may also see this with some of the recommendation engines out there like Amazon and Netflix.

The anti-virus that you rely on can work with this idea as well. Many viruses are going to change over time, and knowing what is going to happen next is hard. These programs are able to learn from the viruses and attacks in the past and use that information in order to block new attacks, even if these attacks are ones that the program did not notice in the past or has never encountered.

Healthcare is a bit option that is going to use machine learning in many cases. For example, it can be used to help us to detect the diseases that someone is going through in some of the earlier stages of the process. It can make a diagnosis of problems just as efficiently as a human but often faster and can help our medical professionals get better at the work that they are doing on a regular basis. It can even come in and help as virtual assistants to make things so much easier overall as well.

These are just a few of the options where we are going to see that machine learning, and some of the features that come with it are going to be useful for businesses throughout all sorts of industries. Many companies are excited to start looking at machine learning and all that it is able to do because there is just so much potential that comes with this kind of programming. When we are able to put it all together, we will find that these are going to be some of the best things that you can do for your business as a whole.

As it stands right now, many experts agree that what we are currently able to do with machine learning is just the tip of the iceberg. It is likely that as more time goes on, we are going to be able to find more and more situations where we would use this kind of technology, and this can really change the way that the world of business works.

Into the Future

Every company that is taking a look at machine learning is going to have its own wishlist for what they would like this to do for them. Wishful thinking, when it is put into action, is eventually something that can come true. In the near future, it is possible to work with machine learning in ways that we never thought possible in the past, and there are often many solutions and uses for this that we would never imagine in the first place. That is just the power of machine learning on its own.

For example, in the future, Adobe would like to be able to add in some more integration between what we are able to do with machine learning and the customer experience. They would like to be able to integrate data streams from social media, apps, websites, and more. This could help them to reach their customers better and really be able to take a more holistic approach when it comes to their marketing campaigns as well.

There is just so much that this kind of technology is going to be able to do for us in the future, and it is important that we learn all of the different ways that we are able to use it for some of our own needs as well. Any business, no matter what industry they are in, will be able to benefit when we work with machine learning and all of the neat things that it is able to do, and we definitely need to spend some of our time learning more about this method and how we are able to use it for some of our own needs as well, whether this helps us to reach your customers, to find new ways of doing business, reducing waste, and so much more.

Chapter 4: The K-Nearest Neighbor Algorithm

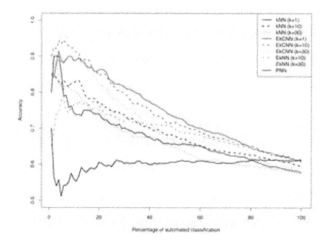

Now that we have had some time to take a look at the machine learning that we will want to work with, and we know more about some of the benefits and more that we are able to do with that machine learning, it is time for us to dive in and learn more about some of the different algorithms that we are able to handle with this kind of process. There are so many different algorithms that are going to fit under the term of machine learning, and the number is growing all of the time as more and more programmers try to jump on board and use this, or find that the available algorithms are not really what they need for that particular project they are focusing on.

The first out of the algorithms that we are going to spend some of our time on will be known as the KNN or the K-Nearest Neighbors algorithm. This is a non-linear classification model, and it is going to be considered one of the supervised machine learning algorithms that we talked about before. This means that the data we have to provide to this algorithm needs to be labeled for us ahead of time or it is not going to work.

When it comes to working with the KNN algorithm, you will find that there are a lot of benefits, and it is going to be able to help you handle a lot of the different projects that you would like. When we are working on this KNN algorithm, you may find that it is really useful when we would like to be able to cut down on some of the noise that is going to sometimes show up in the set of data that you are trying to work with.

Depending on what kind of data you are working with at the time, or how much of it you gathered from a lot of different places over time, and from which sources, you may find that some of the outliers and noise that comes with your data is going to be loud. When we are able to cut down on some of this noise, we will find that it is easier to see the real information that we need inside and will ensure that the results that we are able to get out of any algorithm that we choose to use, but especially the KNN algorithm, is going to be as accurate as possible.

There are many algorithms that we are able to work with when it comes to working with machine learning. This makes it hard to know why you would want to work with this kind of algorithm over some of the others. The benefits of working with the KNN algorithm and why you would want to choose it over some of the other options include:

1. It can work well with problems, even if they are considered multi-class.
2. You are able to apply this algorithm to both problems that are regressive and those that are classification.
3. There aren't any assumptions that come up with the data. This ensures that you get the information that you want, rather than having any assumptions in the place causing some issues.
4. It is an easy algorithm to work with. It is easy to understand, especially if you are brand new to the machine learning process.

However, we will find that there are going to be some more options for some of the algorithms that you are able to choose from because this algorithm, though it has a lot of benefits that go along with it, is not going to work in each situation that you want to use when it comes to machine learning. Along with some of the benefits that we talked about earlier, there are a few negatives of this algorithm and a few situations where you are likely to not want to use this for your needs. Some of the negatives of this algorithm, and why you need to do your research rather than just jumping in and working with this option, include the following:

1. It is going to be computationally and memory-intensive expensive. If you don't have the right system and the right amount of space to work with, it is going to make it more difficult to see the results that you want from this algorithm.
2. If there are a lot of independent variables that you are going to work with, you will find that the KNN algorithm is going to struggle.
3. The KNN algorithm isn't going to work that well if you have any rare event or skewed, target variables.
4. Sensitive to the scale of data.

For any of the problems that we are going to work with, you will find that having a smaller value of k is going to give us more variance in any of the predictions that we are working with. In addition, when you set it so that k is at a bigger value, it is possible that there is going to be more bias in the model as you work on it too.

While you are working with this one though, there may be times when you will need to go through and create some dummy variables. This is going to make it easier to figure out the categorical variables that will show up in this algorithm. This is different than the regressions that we will look for though because you can work with creating the k dummies rather than just the k-1.

With some of this in mind when we start, we then need to make sure that we are finding some of the best methods that will help us to find these values for k in the first place before we get too far. There are a few methods that a programmer is able to use to make this happen, but often, the best option to ensure that the information is accurate and will do what you would like is to work with cross-validation.

Cross-validation is a great process to use, but it is most important because we are able to use this to help us figure out a good estimation of what the error of validation is going to be right from the start, ensuring that we know what to expect and helping us to make some smart decisions when it comes to whether we want to use this algorithm on our data or not. To make sure that this is going to happen in the manner that we want though, we have to make sure that one of the subsets of our training set it withheld from the process when we build up the model so that we can use it for this purpose later on.

Cross-validation is going to be the process where we are able to go through and then divide up the training data in a manner that is as random as possible. For the example that we are going to spend some time talking about here, we are going to work with a validation that is meant to be 10-fold. This means that we are going to take all of the data that we are using for training and then divide it into ten groups.

When we are doing the dividing up, we want to make sure that we are keeping these as close to the same size as we can. From this, about 90 percent of the data that we are using in each set is going to be used to train the model we have. Then the other ten percent, or as close to that as possible when we get started, is going to be used to validate that the model is working and will help us to do some testing before we rely on that model for our business decisions along the way. If we find that the cross-validation is not giving us results that are any good in the process, then this is a sign that we need better data, we need more data for training or that something is wrong with the algorithm.

Another thing that we need to focus on here is the misclassification rate. The one that is the most important to what we are doing in this part is the ten percent that we actually took out of the data for training and held to work on the validation. This procedure is going to be something that we need to go through more than once and repeat to make sure that we are validating all of the work that we are doing here.

Since we are focusing our attention on doing a 10-fold validation, that means that we are planning to go through the cycle ten times. We will train the data with some information in the first set, and then cross-validate it with the data that is held behind in the first place. Then we do the same with the second set, the third set, the fourth set, and all the way through until all of your data is handled. Each of the groups of observations that we decide to work with here and run will be seen as the validation, and then it is also possible to test through this as well to help you get the best results.

As we can see, working with the KNN algorithm is not as difficult as it may seem in the beginning. But it is going to provide us with some awesome ways to learn more about our data and what is inside. And if you go through the process of training and then working with cross-validation along the way, in a manner similar to what we were discussing above, you will find that it is going to provide us with some accurate results in the end, even if it does seem to take a bit longer to go through the training set.

Chapter 5: Creating a Neural Networks

Another option that we are going to spend some time on when it comes to handling our data and making sure that it works out the way that we want is to work with some neural networks. This is another thing that works well with the Scikit-Learn library and will help us to really get the results that we want. These are going to be really strong to work with and can be a neat thing for machine learning because of all the power that comes with them.

To start with, these neural networks are going to work in a similar manner to what we see in the human brain. This will be able to help us to look through data, pick up on some of the different patterns that are there, and more. And when it makes the right predictions, it is able to form some stronger connections and will remember that information in the future as well. And it can even learn from the mistakes and the times when the neural network is not working the way that we would like, then it will be able to learn from that and really make some changes to learn better next time.

Any time that we decide to work with one of these neural networks, we are going to find that there are going to be quite a few layers that will show up with these. And all of these layers are going to take some time to look to see whether there are patterns on this or not. If the network finds that there is a layer where it is able to find a pattern, it will hold onto that before going on to the following layer.

This process is going to continue on through the layers until the neural network is not able to find any more patterns for the process. When it has been able to get to this point, the neural network finds that it is at the end of the job and will use the patterns and more that it has been able to find and will then make a prediction based on that information.

There are going to be a few things that we will be able to find happening at this point in the process. The results that you will get depend on how this program is able to work. If the algorithm that you set up with the neural network went through this process and followed the steps that were above, and then properly sorted through all of the layers, then it will be able to make a good prediction in the process.

If the neural network is accurate with its prediction, then the neurons of the system are going to remember this and will strengthen, ensuring that the neural network will be more accurate the next time it goes through. This is because the program has been able to work with artificial intelligence and machine learning in order to form the strong associations between the object and the patterns. The more times that this system provides us with the right answers, the more efficient it will be when it is time to turn it on and work with it again.

Now, this may seem a little bit far fetched and like it isn't something that could actually happen. But a closer examination of these neural networks will help us to see how they work together and why they are so important. For our example, let's say that your goal is to create a program that is able to take a picture that you input into it, and then, by looking at that picture and going through the layers, the program is able to recognize that the image in that picture is that of a car.

If the program has been set up in the proper manner, it is going to make the right prediction that there is a car in the picture. The program is able to come up with this prediction based on some of the features that it already knows belongs to the car, including the color, the number on the license plate, the placement of the doors, the headlights, and more.

With this one, we need to make sure to remember there is the potential for many layers to show up, but the good news is that the more layers we are able to go through with our images, the more accurate the predictions are going to be overall. If your neural network can make some accurate predictions, then it is going to be able to learn this lesson and will hold onto it along the way and will get faster and more efficient at making the predictions later on.

The next thing that we need to look at when it comes to neural networks is that they are able to remember some of the work that they were able to accomplish in the past. So, if you present the neural network with a picture of a car, and then the neural network is accurate at making a prediction that the image that shows up in the picture was a car, it is able to remember its predictions later similar to what we would see with a human who is learning as well.

Then, later on, if you give the neural algorithm a picture of a car, especially if the second image is similar to the first one that you showed to the algorithm earlier on, it is going to remember the lesson it did before and will use that to make a quick and efficient prediction again. The algorithm will be able to get through the different layers that come with this image quickly and will provide us with a prediction of a car, and it will be able to do this in a lot less time than before. Just think about all of the ways that we would potentially be able to work with this kind of technology, and this algorithm, to make sure that we can learn from the information that we have available already.

Chapter 6: The Linear Classifier Algorithm

As we are working through some of the problems that we want to handle in machine learning, there may be some situations in supervised learning where two of the biggest tasks that you need to spend your time on will need to have some linear classification and linear regression. The linear regression is sometimes going to come into play because it is going to help us to predict some of the value that we have in our data. But then we are also able to work with the linear classifier because it is going to put more attention into some of the classes that are so important with the Python language.

No matter which of these methods you like to use with machine learning, you will be able to do some powerful things with your own coding. In this chapter though, we are going to spend a bit of our time looking at the linear classifier and look at the different steps that you are able to see when it is time to work with this type of machine learning.

To start with though, you will find that the most prevalent type of machine learning that you are able to work with is problems of classification. In fact, a good 80 percent of what you are going to do in machine learning will rely on these classification problems. The main goal that you are going to spend your time on when it comes to classification is to use these algorithms to make a good prediction on how likely it is that a class is actually going to happen, based on the inputs that you use with it, the label, and the class at hand.

If you have a dependent variable or a label and they only come in with two of the classes that you plan to work with from the very beginning, then you know that the algorithm that you are focusing on is going to be a binary classifier. If you would like to work with one of the classifiers but you would like to have it work with more than one class, this means that it is possible for it to tackle any of the labels that have three or more classes at a time. We can explore this a bit later on.

We can take a look at one of the examples of this ahead of time though. Many of the classification problems that we have that we would also say are binary would be able to make a prediction for us about how likely one of our customers will come back and make a second or third purchase after that one. But if you want to take a different angle and would like to see the system make a prediction about the animal type that you place into an image, you will need to work with more of a multiclass kind of classification. This is because it is possible that more than two animal types can show up in the picture that you are working with.

Now we need to take a look at some of the steps that we are able to take in order to measure out our linear classifier performance. Accuracy is always going to be important when we are working in machine learning because it will ensure that we are actually getting the results that we need when we rely on them. The performance of this kind of classifier overall is going to be measured with the accuracy metric, and that should show us just how important this metric is going to be.

When we take a look at the accuracy though, it is going to be a good measurement of whether or not our algorithm is able to take in the right values and then divide that number by how many observations are actually present in your work. The higher the accuracy that we are able to get here, the better it is for some of our work and what we can rely on out of this algorithm.

We can take a look at how this is going to work. For example, if you are setting up the value of accuracy to be a minimum of 85 percent, this means that the algorithm will need to be right 85 percent of the time. On the other hand, this same algorithm is going to end up being wrong about 15 percent of the time. If you are working with numbers and plan to use the data you have to make some good predictions, then it is important that your accuracy ends up being as high as possible.

As we look more at the accuracy, we need to keep in mind that there can be some shortcomings with this kind of metric. This is always going to show up when you take a look at the class of imbalance. A data set that is not balanced all that well is going to occur when the observations that you have in the algorithm isn't able to equal all of the groups that you are using in this as well.

To help us get a better understanding of how this is going to work, we can say that we are focusing our attention on the challenge of classifying a rare event using some logistics. In this case, we would need to take some time to think about the classifier that is the best to work with, and that would include something like estimating how many patients passed on maybe when they were in contact with a specific disease. In the data that you are presented with, you may find that the set tells you that about five percent of the patients who contracted this disease died from it.

With this information in mind, you would then be able to bring in the linear classifier algorithm and train it so that it was able to predict how many deaths are likely to happen from the general population if they get the disease, and even make predictions on who is the most likely to die if they caught the disease. This metric of accuracy is then going to be in order to help us evaluate the performance of a hospital or clinic. If the average of deaths of patients who die from this disease is 5 percent, and a hospital is at two percent, then their performance is doing well. But if the average of a hospital is at

10 percent, then there may need to be some changes to prevent as many deaths from this disease.

The other thing that we need to focus on next is going to be something that we can call the confusion matrix. This is going to be one of the better ways that we are able to look at how a classifier is able to perform compared to some of the accuracies that we had above. This matrix is going to help us to see how our classifier will perform when we can compare it to the accuracy that we had above. When you decide to bring in our confusion matrix, you will start to get a good visual about the classifier and its accuracy by comparing the predicted, and the actual, classes to one another.

Keep in mind with this one that the confusion matrix that turns out to be binary is going to consist of squares. If you decide that this is the matrix that you would like to work with, there are a few parts that can come with it including the following:

1. TP: This is going to be known as the true positive. This is going to contain all of the predicted values that were correctly predicted as an actual positive.
2. FP: This is going to be the false ones or the ones that were predicted in an incorrect manner. They were usually predicted as positive, but they were

actually negative. This means that the negative values show up, but they had been predicted ahead of time as positive.

3. FN: This is a false negative. This is when your positive values were predicted as negative.

4. TN: This is going to be the true negative. These are the values that were predicted in a correct manner and were predicted as actual negative.

When you have a programmer who is able to take a look at this kind of matrix and can use it in the proper manner, they are going to end up with a ton of information to work with. The confusion matrix is going to help us to really look at the predicted class, and compare it over to the actual class that we get, to help us compare and contrast what is going on with that data as well.

The final thing that we need to take a look at here is whether or not the precision and the sensitivity is going to be important with some of the work that we will do. The confusion matrix is going to end up being one of the best things that we can focus on when it is time to look at our linear classifications and when we want to gain a better understanding of the information that our data is holding onto.

But when we do decide to work with this kind of matrix, you will find that it opens up the door to a ton of information showing up along the way. These matrices are worth the time though because they will provide you with a lot of information, especially when we are looking at the false and true positives inside of some of the information that we have. However, even though this is a great thing for us to work with, there will be some cases when it is better to work on a metric that is more concise so that we can better understand whatever information we are going through.

To help us get through this a bit more, we need to take a closer look at the metric that we would like to use. And the first metric is precision. This is an important metric to spend our time on because it will really show us how accurate our class will be. This may not make a lot of sense, but it basically means that the precision metric is really going to help us to get a measure of how likely the positive class prediction is going to turn out correct in the long run. The formula that we are able to run to show this will include:

Precision = TP / (TP + FP)

The maximum score that we are going to have when we do this will show up here. And this is going to show us the classifier and be right when we have a positive value in place. While precision and a good look at how precise one of our metrics is before we start are important to our success, it is not going to be the only metric that we want to spend our time on at all. We also want to spend some time taking a look at how sensitive the metric is as well.

This sensitivity is going to be important because it is going to let us know how much the ratio of the positive classes in the algorithm is and how often they can make the accurate predictions that you are looking for. This is a good metric to work with because it is going to help us to take a look at the positive formula that is there and can make sure that we will be able to check whether things are lining up in the manner that we want. If you would like to check what the sensitivity of your algorithm is ahead of time, then you will need to work with the following formula to help:

Recall = TP / (TP + FN)

Chapter 7: Working with Recurrent Neural Networks

When we were doing some work earlier on in this guidebook, remember that we did bring up the topic of neural networks and all of the neat things that they will be able to do for us to get the work done. Remember that these neural networks are going to be on a kind of learning curve. What this means is that when they are able to provide us with the right answer, the connections that are there will grow stronger, which allows them to make better predictions based on the information that they in the past, to make stronger predictions.

What this means for us is that these neural networks are able to work in a manner that is similar to how the human learns and remembers things. This can make it a stronger and much more efficient method to work with overall, especially when it comes to how it is able to handle some of the decisions that it makes later on. And when it has some time to learn and do more work, the neural network is going to get so much better at making some of the good predictions that we need.

Now that we have some of that information down, it is time for us to go back a bit and look more at these neural networks, and get a better understanding of how they are going to work in mimicking the learning that the human brain is able to do.

The first thing that we are able to handle here is how the brain is going to work. You may notice from your own experience that the brain is not going to be in the habit of restarting its thinking patterns every few seconds. If this were true, then it would be impossible for any of us to accomplish anything or learn anything very well.

The brain is able to work, and we are able to progress and learn because we have the ability to build up anything that we were able to learn about in the past. This past could be as recent as a few minutes ago, or it could be some of the things that we were able to learn as a child. As we go through some of the different parts that we learned about in this guidebook, it is likely that you understand the patterns and the words and some of the ideas, based on what we explored earlier on. This is how we are able to really put it all together and see some amazing progress in the process.

This is going to be important because it is going to show us that the thoughts and some of the different parts of learning that we gain are going to stick with us when we work with persistence and consistency. This is going to be the idea that we are able to use when it is time to work on the recurrent neural network. In most situations, the neural network that we explored in an earlier chapter will not be able to get all of this done for us, and honestly, that is often one of the reasons that people may not like to use it, especially with some of the paths that machine learning is going to do in the future.

There are a few methods that we can use to help us think about it. First, if you would like to be able to take some events and then classify them based on what happens inside of a movie, for example, it is going to be hard to get a traditional form of the neural network to reason through this option. The reason with this one is that the neural network is not going to be able to remember all of the parts that show up in the code in this manner.

The neat thing that we are going to see with this one though is that we are able to bring in the recurrent neural network to help us address this big problem when we are working in machine learning. The recurrent neural network is going to be pretty similar to what we see with the traditional neural network, but it is going to focus more on being a loop, which allows the information to stick around after the network has been able to learn about it.

With this kind of neural network, the loop that you see is going to allow any of the information that is on the network to be learned and then will pass from one part of the network over to another one as needed. This is going to be an idea that is pretty similar to having more than one copy of your network, and then each of the messages that you need will move down the line in a pattern as well.

The chain nature that we are going to see here is able to help us to reveal that these kinds of the network will be related back to a list and a sequence in many situations. They are also going to be an architecture type that is pretty natural for neural networks so that they are able to use the data that they want. And we have to work with these on a regular basis to keep them sharp and working in the manner that we would like.

Over the past few years, there has been a lot of success when we are able to take the methods of these networks and adding them to machine learning. And in the process, we are able to use this kind of method in order to help us handle a lot of different types of machine learning like automatic translation, image captioning, modeling of languages, and speech recognition.

As we take a look back at some of the neural networks that we spent our time on earlier, we are going to see that there is a big limitation when it comes to having a lot of constraints that are on the API that we use. These constraints are likely going to only take a vector that provides them with an input that is known ahead of time, and then they are going to only be able to produce a vector that is fixed in size when we use the output. Keep in mind that this is just the beginning of the issues and problems that we are going to be able to work with when we choose the recurrent neural network for some of our needs.

To make it a little bit easier for us to see how the recurrent neural network is going to work for our needs, and why they are going to be better for us to work with when it comes to these networks compared to the traditional methods, we will need to take a look at the chart that we have above to make sure we can handle all of this. When we look at that chart, we are going to see that each part is going to have a few rectangles that we need to focus on, and we can look at each of these parts as one of the vectors that we will focus on. And then the arrows that we see in between all of these can help us to see what will happen in the functions and which direction they are supposed to take.

When it is time for us to input the vectors, we are going to be able to distinguish these vectors away from the other options because they are going to show up in red. Then the output vectors are going to be brought up inside of this and will be in blue this time. Then there is a third color in this graph, which is the green vectors and those will hold onto the state of the RNN.

Taking a closer look at the chart that is above, and helping us to read it from left to right, we are able to see how all of the parts are going to work in our recurrent neural network, and why all of these are so important to some of the things that we want to work wit:

1. The first part that we will want to work with is the processing mode that is vanilla. This one means that we not going to focus on the RNN at all. This is going to mean that the input we are working with will end up being fixed, along with the output. We can call this one the image classification as well.

2. Then we are able to work with the sequence output. This second part is going to be the image captioning that we are going to be taken with an image, and then, when it has had some time to look at the image, it is going to provide us with some words to describe what is going on.

3. The sequence input is going to be the third part that we need to focus on. This is going to fall into the third picture that we have above and it is seen more like the analysis that is sentimental because it is going to show us the sentence that is given, and then will help us to figure out whether the sentiment that is used with it is positive or negative in the process.

4. We then need to take a look at the sequence output and input. You will find that this one is going to be shown off in the fourth box. It is going to be similar to what we find with machine translation and it is when the RNN that we have is able to read out a sentence in the English language. Then it is able to take some of the information and will give us an output that is able to read out the sentence in another language like French.

5. And then we are able to take a look at the last and final box that is present in all of this. This one is going to be the synced sequence input and output that we are able to work with. A good example of this one is going to be the video classification and it is a good one to help us when we want to label out all of the frames that are going to occur in a video if we decide that we would like to work with it in this manner.

When we have had some time to go through and check all of this out, we can then double-check whether the constraints that we need are in place or if they are missing. If you did this well, you will see that some of the constraints that will talk about the lengths of the sequences we would like to list out ahead of time are not going to be there. The reason that we see this is that the recurrent transformation, or the part that we will see with the green rectangles, will be fixed during this process. This is a good thing because it allows us to apply it as often as we would like in order to get things to work.

It is now time to take some of this information and look at how we are able to work with it in the RNN or focus on the green parts of our chart above. This is where we need to make sure that the RNN is trained in the right mode. Basically, we are using the character-level language model, which means that we are going to be able to supply this with a lot of text and data, and then, once it has had a chance to look at and hopefully learn from the data, we are going to request that it does something for us.

This is also the step where we would want the neural network to model the probability of the distribution of the character that is going to show up next when we have a sequence going on. And this can happen with the RNN if we base it on the sequence that we provided into it during training. This is going to help us to show up with some new text, or it can help us when it is time to do decoding, even if you do plan to just work with one of these characters at a time.

We can take a look at a good example of how this is going to work for our needs. Let's say that we are starting out with vocabulary in a new language that is limited, and we only have four letters that are possible to work with, the four letters of the helo. With this kind of information, we want to make sure that the RNN can be trained to do a training sequence so that it is able to list out "hello" instead of the other option. This sequence is going to be a source of four different training models that we are able to put together to ensure that we are going to get things to work the way that we want, even if we are only able to input or receive one character out of this at a time.

This is going to seem complex to work with, but you will find that when we go through it one step at a time, and see how this is supposed to work, we will be able to get all of it to work, and you will soon recognize how this is going to help us out in the long run. Some of the different parts that we need to look at here and consider along the way to get things done are the following:

1. The probability of getting "e" should be just as likely to occur as getting the letter "h".
2. "L should be likely in the context of "he"
3. The "l" should also be likely if the system is given the context of "hel"
4. "o" should be likely if the other sequences have happened and the context of "hell" is in place.

This means that we are going to be ready to encode all of the characters that show up in our vector, and we need to work with the l of k in coding. This is done because it is going to help us to get all zeroes except for a single one at the index of the character in the vocabulary. With this information, we need to find a way to feed them in so the RNN can read them, doing the characters one at a time, and then we can use the right functions to help out with this.

Once we have been able to go through the steps above and gotten the text to show up in the order that we would like, we need to spend some time doing the observations that are needed on the sequence of the output vectors in 4-D. One of these dimensions is going to be with each of the characters that we are hoping to show up in all of this. We are then able to interpret this in a manner based on the confidence that we want to place in this system, and how well we think the neural network is going to be able to come in and assign the characters at the right time and int eh right order.

The diagram that we are able to see below is going to show us a better idea of how this kind of distribution is supposed to work for us:

Out of this, we may use an example of seeing that in the first time step, the RNN would see the character of "h" it was able to assign some confidence to this of 1.0, to the next letter turning into "h", 2.2 to getting the letter "e" -3.0 to "l" "and 4.1 to "o". Since the training data that we are using, (which is the string of hello that we talked about above), had the next right character being "e" we want to increase the confidence or the green color, and then decrease how confident it is in all of the other letters, which are going to be shown in the red above.

In addition to some of the information that we are going to see here, there is going to be an additional step that we are able to go through that will help us to get to the desired character target out of the four that we are able to work with here as well. And we want to make sure that we have a lot of confidence before we ever use it that the network is able to handle this kind of work.

This step is going to be a bit harder to handle compared to some of the others, but it is something that we need to focus some of our attention on because the more confidence that we are able to add into this, the easier it is to see that the system or the algorithm will be able to get the results that we want as the output.

So, since we are working on the process of making sure the RNN behaves properly, and this means that it is going to have some operations that are differentiable along the way, we first need to bring in one of the algorithms that we are using here for the process of backpropagation.

This is something that may sound a bit confusing and hard to work in the first place, but basically, it is going to be known as the recursive application of the chain rule that you may have heard about before when you did calculus. The reason that we are going to focus on this is that it helps us to find the right direction to take for adjusting all of the weights in the information. This helps us to increase the scores in the targets that we want while leaving everything else the same.

Then we are able to go through and work on updating the parameters. This is going to be something that we need to work with because it takes all of our weights along the way and will nudge them up a bit so that they go in the direction that we need to make this work. If it is possible, it is best to double-check all of the inputs that we are using to help ensure that we can feed them into the RNN and still get everything to end up even when we are all done. And then when the parameter is able to finish the update, you should find that the score of all the characters will fit inline the way so that you get the right answers.

Now, keep in mind that when you run this the first time, it may not be as accurate as you would like. This means that we will need to go through this process a few times to help make sure that all of the accuracy and precision that we want to work with will be there. This is a frustrating thing in some cases because it is not going to be as clear-cut as we might like as a beginner and there will not be a set number of times when we will need to do this. You have to consider the data points that you are working with, and how complex the situation is as well, and then go from there until the accuracy is right.

So, let's say that we start out with something simple like the "hello" code that we had earlier in this chapter. With a code that is this simple, it is not going to take too long to get the

RNN to work and get the confidence that is needed ahead of time. But if you are taking these same ideas and trying to have it decade a large book or a ton of words, then this one, of course, is going to take more tries and more energy in order to accomplish.

As we start to work with these neural networks more and more, you are going to eventually get to the time of testing. This is important because it is going to provide us with some of the certainty that we need to know that we are feeding in the characters necessary to this algorithm. And once we have been able to feed these characters into the system, then it is time to make sure that the distribution you are working with will describe which characters your system is able to bring out next. As you work on this program we should take a few moments to look it over to see whether it is doing this well and providing you the right information before you proceed and waste more time when things are not going well.

Now, if you are doing the steps above and find that your algorithm is not providing you with the answers that you would like the first time around, which is possible, this just means that you need to work on it a bit and train it some more ahead of time to get it to work. It does not mean that the RNN failed and that you should never work with it again. This is an algorithm that is able to learn as it goes, so if you find that it is not providing you with the answers that you would like, then you just need to go through the process a few more times to get it all set up and ready to go. You will need to do this as many times as it takes in order to make sure that the neural network is going to behave in the way that you would like.

We spent quite a bit of time in this chapter taking a look at these recurrent neural networks and all of the things that they are able to do to help us get the work done and see some of the results that we would like as well. But some of the coding that we are able to do with them, and the way that they can help us to work on our networks and see some results from our data, is amazing and it is so important to learn how to make these work for some of our needs.

The RNN algorithm is going to be really powerful and it is able to provide us with a lot of the answers that we need to our common machine learning questions, often at a better rate than we are able to use with the other algorithms that are out there. When you are ready to work with this kind of algorithm for some of your own needs, make sure to go through some of the steps that we have above and see how this is going to be able to benefit you as well.

Chapter 8: Clustering Algorithms

While we are learning more about machine learning and some of the neat things that you are able to do with all of this, it is time for us to take a look at the algorithm known as the K-Means clustering. This is going to be one that shows up quite a bit and can help you to get more accomplished with the coding that you do. The basic idea that comes with this one is that you are able to take the data from the system, all of it that we have not been able to label yet, and then we are going to put it together into some clusters to see what is going on.

The main goal that we are going to see when we handle some of these clusters is that the objects that all into the same cluster with one another are going to be related to one another closely and they will not come in with as many similarities to the options that fall into the other clusters that you have. The similarity that you see with the items that are in the same clusters is going to be the metric that we are able to use to see how strong the relationship between the objects of data can be.

The field of data mining is then able to work with the algorithm of clustering quite a bit. This is going to be really true if you are going to do some kind of exploration. But this is not going to be the only kind of field that will see some benefit from this algorithm. It is also possible to use it in some fields like information retrieval, data compression, pattern recognition, image analysis and so much more.

The K-Means clustering algorithm is also going to work and form some clusters that we would like, based on how similar the values that you have in the data are to one another. You can then go through and specify what you would like to see with the values of K, which will simply be how many clusters you are hoping to work with here and how many parts you want to try and split the data into. This depends on what you are hoping to get out of it. If you just want to sort through the males and females who shop at your store, you only need two clusters. If you want to sort out into more you can do that as well.

This clustering algorithm is going to start out by helping us figure out what value will be the center of all our clusters and then it is going to go through a total of three other steps to help make this happen including:

1. You will want to start with the Euclidian distance between each data instance and the centroids for all of the clusters.
2. Assign the instances of data to the cluster of centroid with the nearest distance possible.

3. Calculate the new centroid values, depending on the mean values of the coordinates of the data instances from the corresponding cluster.

Now to work with this kind of algorithm, the input that we really need to look for to make the k-means happen is going to be found in the matrix for X. We are then able to go through this and check on the organization that is present for any choices to ensure that the rows you create are different samples each time, while each of the columns that you want to work with are going to have different factors as you work with them. If you are able to do this, you will only have to work with two steps to get it all done.

For our first step, we have to really consider the centers that we want to have for all of our clusters. The more of these clusters that we want to work with, the longer that this will take. If you are looking through the data and you are not that sure where to put the centers, then you may want to start out with some points that are more random and then see what happens with it. If things are not matching up in the manner that you would like with the help of this method, then you can always go through and try out a different center later on.

Then we can move on to the second step, and that is where we need to focus on the main loop. After you have had some time to work with the chosen centers, then you are able to decide where the data points will fit and which clusters they should work with as well. you can look at all of the samples that you have in order to figure out where to place these.

From this point in the game, we will need to spend some time on our recalculations to move around the centers of those clusters again. This time it needs to be based on the original points that each one was assigned. To make all of this happen, you just need to grab the samples that you have and figure out what the mean is on these as well. As soon as you get an answer for this one, then you will have your k-means ready to go.

This is not the end though. It is likely that we will need to head through these steps a few times before the convergence that this algorithm is looking for actually happens. For the most part though, based on the data amount that you have and where you are starting out, this can be done in five steps, and sometimes less. But if you are working on a complex problem with a lot of parts and there are many points of data that have a big variance, then it is possible that more steps are going to need to happen.

With this in mind though, we need to take a look at some of the coding that we are able to do in order to make this work for some of our needs as well. To start with here, we are going to look at how we are able to add in the k-means to the process. But this is going to bring up the question of how we are supposed to make all of this happen so that we can find the k-means and create the clusters that we would like along the way.

One thing to keep in mind while we go through this is that the Euclidean distance is going to be important, and then we also need to focus on the cost of the functions put together to give us the results that we want. To make this easier, we need to take a look at some of the coding that will take over for this one. The best code to work with here to make all of this work will include:

```
import numpy as np
import matplotlib.pyplot as plt

def d(u, v):
 diff = u - v
 return diff.dot(diff)

def cost(X, R, M):
 cost = 0
 for k in xrange(len(M)):
  for n in xrange(len(X)):
```

```
cost += R[n,k]*d(M[k], X[n])
return cost
```

Take a moment to type this into your compiler to see how it is going to work for your needs as well. Once this is in the compiler and you have been able to go through and define the function in a manner so that the algorithm is going to plot out the results you are set to go. The plots will show up on the graph that you have, and it is going to basically turn into a scatterplot of information. There will be a few colors that are there because this will help us to notice the differences in the dots that we have and can make it easier to figure out the membership of the information that is found in each one. The coding to make this happen is easier than it may seem, and is going to include the following:

```
def plot_k_means(X, K, max_iter=20, beta=1.0):
N, D = X.shape
M = np.zeros((K, D))
R = np.ones((N, K)) / K

# initialize M to random
for k in xrange(K):
M[k] = X[np.random.choice(N)]

grid_width = 5
```

```
grid_height = max_iter / grid_width
random_colors = np.random.random((K, 3))
plt.figure()

costs = np.zeros(max_iter)
for i in xrange(max_iter):
# moved the plot inside the for loop
colors = R.dot(random_colors)
plt.subplot(grid_width, grid_height, i+1)
plt.scatter(X[:,0], X[:,1], c=colors)

# step 1: determine assignments / resposibilities
# is this inefficient?
for k in xrange(K):
for n in xrange(N):
R[n,k] = np.exp(-beta*d(M[k], X[n])) / np.sum( np.exp(-
beta*d(M[j], X[n])) for j in xrange(K) )

# step 2: recalculate means
for k in xrange(K):
M[k] = R[:,k].dot(X) / R[:,k].sum()

costs[i] = cost(X, R, M)
if i > 0:
if np.abs(costs[i] - costs[i-1]) < 10e-5:
break
```

plt.show()

Notice that when we are working with this kind of code above, the M and the R are going to stand out with their own matrices. To start, we can look at the R. This one is going to be found in a brand new matrix because it is going to hold onto the two indices that you need, namely the k and the n.

This doesn't mean that we can ignore what is going to happen with the M though. This one is going to be a matrix on its own as well. this is because it is going to include what is known as the D-dimensional vectors that come with K. The variable that will be considered the variable here is going to be responsible for helping us control how fuzzy, close together, or spread out the memberships of the clusters are. These will also be known as the hyperparameters that we discuss in other parts of this guidebook.

From all of this information, we will be able to go through and create a new main function that is able to create some of the rando clusters that we have, and then can call up the functions that we were able to define above. We are able to use a bit of Python coding to help us get this done, and this will include the following:

def main():

```
# assume 3 means
D = 2 # so we can visualize it more easily
s = 4 # separation so we can control how far apart the
means are
mu1 = np.array([0, 0])
mu2 = np.array([s, s])
mu3 = np.array([0, s])


N = 900 # number of samples
X = np.zeros((N, D))
X[:300, :] = np.random.randn(300, D) + mu1
X[300:600, :] = np.random.randn(300, D) + mu2
X[600:, :] = np.random.randn(300, D) + mu3


# what does it look like without clustering?
plt.scatter(X[:,0], X[:,1])
plt.show()


K = 3 # luckily, we already know this
plot_k_means(X, K)


# K = 5 # what happens if we choose a "bad" K?
# plot_k_means(X, K, max_iter=30)


# K = 5 # what happens if we change beta?
# plot_k_means(X, K, max_iter=30, beta=0.3)
```

```
if __name__ == '__main__':
    main()
```

We can already see from all of this that the Python language can take a task that seems pretty complicated and will divide it up in a manner that makes life a bit easier to handle and use as well. With the codes that we have been able to work within this chapter, we are basically setting it up so that we have our own k-means algorithm, and you should now have a much better understanding of how all of this is going to work.

You can now add in some data, with the help of the compiler that you are working with and the codes above and see what is going to happen when you work through all of this process as well. try out a few of these along the way and see how they work, and what you are able to do to make them work for your needs, and see how great they will be when creating some of the clusters that you would like with your data as well.

Chapter 9: Decision Trees and Turning Them Into Random Forests

Another option that we are able to take a look at when it comes to working with machine learning and all of the neat things that we are able to do with this kind of learning is going to be the decision trees and random forests. These kinds of algorithms are going to go together pretty well, and learning how to make them work for some of our own needs as well is going to be one of the best ways to ensure that we are able to get them to provide us with the answers that we need along the way.

Often we are going to find that the random forest and the decision tree are going to be found in the same kinds of topics in machine learning and that both of these algorithms are going to be able to work well together. These are going to be some efficient data tools that are able to help us to take on two of the choices that we would like to work with, and sometimes even more than two choices, especially when our choices are quite a bit different, and then we will use this information to help us figure out which decision out of the two (or more), that is going to be the best for your business and what you would like to be able to do in the future.

When you are looking at the future of your business and what you would like to do overall, it is possible that you will be presented with more than one option at a time. And sometimes, even though those options may be very different from one another, you will see that they are all good options and something that you would consider doing. But since you are only able to pick one because of them being so different or because of limited resources, you need to pick out a method that will help you to choose.

This is where the decision tree is going to come into play here. It is able to take your choices and then make some predictions on the outcomes of each one. When you are able to glance at these and see what the most likely outcome of each decision is, you can take out some of the risks that you will find with some of your decisions, and can actually choose the one that is right for you.

Now, you will find that there are a few different ways that you are able to work with these decision trees. Many of those who are working with machine learning will use it if either of their variables is categorical and one is random. However, there are times when you will need to use these decision trees with some of the classification problems that you have. To ensure that you are picking out and creating your decision tree well, then you need to make sure that you take all of the sets of data that you have and then split them up to be in two or more sets, with some similar data in each one. You can then sort this out with the help of independent variables because it will help you to set it up the way that the decision tree needs.

Sometimes, these decision trees are not going to end up acting in the manner that we need and sometimes it is better to take this out a bit more and work with two or more decision trees together. This is when the decision tree is technically going to switch over to a different type of algorithm that we are able to work with, and this one is going to be known as a random forest. Basically, the random forest is just going to be a collection of decision trees that we want to focus on.

The random forest algorithm is going to be a popular option to work with because they will help you to take a closer look at a lot of decisions that you may need to make for your business, and then will help you to see all of the possible outcomes of each one. You are then able to take a look at these and decide which decision is the best one for you.

As you can imagine already, there are going to be a lot of different applications that you will find when it comes to these random forests. This is because the random forest is going to be perfect when it is time for you to really take a look at some important decisions that you want to make, and then will help you to see the outcomes and choose based on this information. And often these random forests are going to do a great job at providing us with a clear-cut picture of our predictions and insights compared to some of the other options. Some of the ways that we are able to take on these random forests and get them to work in the manner that we would like includes:

- When you are working on your own training sets, you will find that all of the objects that are inside a set will be generated randomly, and it can be replaced if your random tree things that this is necessary and better for your needs.
- If there are M input variable amounts, then m<M is going to be specified from the beginning, and it will be held as a constant. The reason that this is so important because it means that each tree that you have is randomly picked from their own variable using M.
- The goal of each of your random trees will be to find the split that is the best for the variable m.
- As the tree grows, all of these trees are going to keep getting as big as they possibly can. Remember that these random trees are not going to prune themselves.
- The forest that is created from a random tree can be great because it is much better at predicting certain outcomes. It is able to do this for you because it will take all prediction from each of the trees that you create and then will be able to select the average for regression or the consensus that you get during classification.

Random forests are a good tool that a programmer is able to use when they would like to make sure that they add in some data science to the machine learning that you are doing, and there are going to be many benefits. But any time that you are looking for an easy way to look through some of the options that are available for your work, and you want help making some smart decisions, then the decision trees and random forests will be the best option for you to choose.

As we can see here, there are a lot of times when we are going to be able to benefit from working with the random forests, and even with a simple decision tree if you are focused on just a few decisions rather than many. These both are going to help you to see the most likely outcome of a situation and can make it easier for you to really make sure that you understand what is going on with your options and choices at the time.

If these are set up and working in the proper manner, you will find that it is an easier way to see what is likely to happen based on the decision that you make, and it can lead you to make decisions that are based on facts and figures and data, rather than ones based on emotions and uncertainty. And we can all agree that this is going to be much better for the success of your business overall.

Chapter 10: The Support Vector Machines

While we are on the topics of some of the different algorithms that you are able to use when you work with machine learning, and how all of these are able to help us learn more about our data and what we are able to do with all of that data, it is time to take a look at the support vector machines, or the SVM. These are going to be the algorithms that we are able to use when we would like to take the data set that we are working with, and then plot all of the data so that they are able to show up on a plot that is n-dimensional. N is going to be all of the features that you are going to show on the chart as well.

It is possible for the programmer to go through and take on the value of these features, and work in order to translate all of this over to the value that you would use for some of your own chosen coordinates. The job that you are going to be able to do when it is time to get through to this point is to really learn where the hyperplane will fall. Sometimes, there are more than one of these hyperplanes to work with, and you need to make sure that you find the right one. The reason for this is that it is really able to show you what a difference there will be when we look at the classes that show up.

As we just mentioned, it is possible that you will find more than one of these support vectors showing up on your graphs in some cases. The good news with this though, so that you don't get too worried about it, is that not all of the vectors that you find are going to be important and you can usually tell which ones are important and which ones are not, with just a glance. Often, many of the vectors that you will see will just point to the coordinates of the individual observations that you are able to see there.

From this point then, you are able to work with the SVM algorithm in order to turn into the frontier, the part that is able to separate all of the different vectors that you have into classes, and then you will find the line that will need to be your hyperplane. And at this point, there are going to be two main parts that we will need to focus our attention on the most in order to get the results that we want.

Now, up until we got to this point, some of the different steps that we were talking about and looking through may seem a bit confusing, and you may worry that you will not be able to use this algorithm because of it. That is why we are going to take a detour here a bit and learn how we are able to get this to help us sort out our data and ensure that we see the best results.

First, we have to make sure that when we work with the SVM, that we are going to be able to find the hyperplane that will make all of this work the way that we would like. After you get some experience with this one, you will find that it is easier to get that hyperplane. But for a beginner, this is hard and it is possible that there will be two or more hyperplanes that are trying to get your attention at the same time as well.

This fact, that we are going to work with more than one hyperplane that we have to sort through is sometimes a big challenge for the beginner. You want to make sure that you are choosing the right hyperplane for the work that you want to do, rather than picking out the wrong one and then making all of the data fit it when it is not right.

The good thing to remember here is that even if you do have a few options when it comes to hyperplanes, there are still going to be some easy steps that we are able to use to help us pick out the right one. The specific steps that you are able to use when trying to figure out the hyperplane for your SVM will include:

·   We are going to start out with three hyperplanes that we will call 1, 2, and 3. Then we are going to spend time figuring out which hyperplane is right so that we can classify the star and the circle.

- The good news is there is a pretty simple rule that you can follow so that it becomes easier to identify which hyperplane is the right one. The hyperplane that you want to go with will be the one that segregates your classes the best.
- That one was easy to work with, but in the next one, our hyperplanes of 1, 2, and 3 are all going through the classes and they segregate them in a manner that is similar. For example, all of the lines or these hyperplanes are going to run parallel with each other. From here you may find that it is hard to pick which hyperplane is the right one.
- For the issue that is above, we will need to use what is known as the margin. This is basically the distance that occurs between the hyperplane and the nearest data point from either of the two classes. Then you will be able to get some numbers that can help you out. These numbers may be closer together, but they will point out which hyperplane is going to be the best.

You will find that these support vector machines are going to be good options to spend some time on overall. They will help us to really get some of the work done that we would like and ensures that we are really able to handle the insights and predictions in a manner that is accurate and easy to understand as well.

Chapter 11: How to Work with Validation and Optimization Techniques

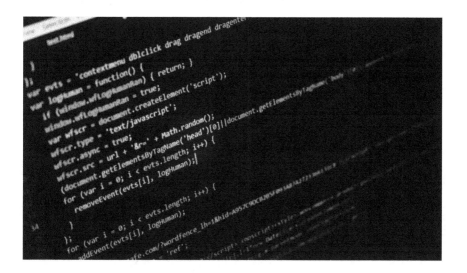

Now that we have had some time to look at some of the amazing techniques and algorithms that are available with machine learning, it is time for us to really get into some of the work that we are able to do to ensure these algorithms are smart and will work in the manner that we would like. In this chapter, we are going to take some time to look through the validation of an algorithm to make sure that it behaves the way that we would like. And from there we will be able to focus on how to optimize the techniques that we are focusing on so that they provide us with the best insights and predictions possible, and so we are actually able to get some good information out of them as well.

This is a lot to take in right from the start so we are going to take some time to talk about the different validation and optimization techniques that are out there, and what we are able to do with them to help us see the best results.

Techniques for Cross-Validation

The first validation technique that we are going to spend some time looking at in this chapter is going to be the cross-validation. With this one, we are going to take the algorithms of machine learning and then take our set of data and ensure that it is divided up into three parts. We will have the first part of the data be for training our algorithm, the second part for validating the algorithm, and then the third and final part is going to be used to test the algorithm and ensure it is working well.

The first set of data that we need to take a look at here when we are exploring some of the things that we can do with machine learning is the training set. This training set is going to be the part that we use to take our algorithm and rain it to behave the way that we would like. We will usually want to put about 60 percent of the data that we have available to work on training the model to make sure that it is going to work the way that you would like.

Then we are going to work with the data set that handles the validation. Once we have been able to select out a model that can perform well with the training set, it is time to run the model with our validation set. This is going to be a small subset of the data, and it is usually going to range from 10 to 20 percent of the data that you have. this set is going to help us with these models because it is going to give us an evaluation, without bias, of the fitness of the model. If the error on the data set for validation increases, then it is possible that we are working with a model that overfits.

And finally, we have the test data set. This is going to be new data that has never been used in the training at all. This is going to be a bit smaller but it is going to contain about 5 to 20 percent of the set of data that we have. and it is meant to help us test out the model evaluation that we are working on to see whether it is accurate or not.

In some cases, there is going to only be a training and a test set, and the programmer is not going to work with any validation set. There are some issues with this one though. Due to the sample variability between the test set and the training, the model is going to provide us with a better prediction on the data that we train but will fail to generalize on the test data. This can make us deal with a low error rate during training, but a high rate of an error on the testing phase of this process.

When we are able to go through and split up the sets of data that we have into the training test, and the validation set that we need, it is time to work with just one of the subsets of the data. Then it is possible to train this with fewer observations of the model. This helps when some of the subsets are not going to perform well, and then when this happens, we will see that it provides us with an overestimated test error rate for the model that is trying to get the whole set of to fit on that model you created.

To help us to solve both of these issues, we are going to work through this with an approach that is known as cross-validation. This is going to be one of the statistical techniques that will help us to partition the data so that it goes into subsets, which will allow us a way to train the data on one of the subsets. Then the rest of the data is going to be used to help us evaluate how well the model was able to perform and whether or not it did the work in the manner that we would like.

Now, to make sure that we are able to handle some of this work a little bit easier, and to ensure that we can reduce the amount of variability that will show up in this kind of data, we may go through and perform a lot of rounds of this cross-validation. But we will need to make sure that we are doing with this a new subset of the same data each time. We are then able to combine the validation results that we get out of these rounds so that we are going to get a better estimated of the predictive performance that we will get out of this model.

When we are doing with this, the cross-validation that we are focusing on is going to be able to provide us back with an estimate of the performance of that model, telling us which one is going to be the most accurate, compared to just doing this training one time and making an assumption that it is going to work the way that we want.

This may seem like a lot of information to keep track of right now, and it is a lot to hold onto. But with some of this information in mind, there are going to be a few techniques that we are going to see when it is time to bring out cross-validation, and some of these include:

1. Leave one out cross-validation or LOOCV: IN this one, we are going to take our set of data and divide it into two pairs to work on. In the first part, we are going to have a single observation, which is going to be the test data. And then in the second one, we are going to have all of the other observations that come in our set of data, and these will form up our training data.

a. There are a few advantages to working with this one. First, we are going to find that there is far less bias because we are going to use all of the set of data for training compared to some of the validation set approach where we are only working with part of the data to help with training.

b. There isn't going to be any randomness in the training or the test data because we will perform this many times and it will still give us the same results.

c. There are some disadvantages that come with this one as well. For example, MSE is going to vary as the test data is going to work with just one single observation. This sometimes adds some variability to the work. If the data point that you work with ends up being an outlier, then you will find that the variability is going to be much higher.

d. The execution of this model is going to be more expensive than some other options because the model has to be fitted n times rather than just once or twice.

2. K Fold cross-validation: This is going to be a technique of cross-validation that is going to take the set of data and randomly divide it into k groups

or folds that are similar in size. The first fold that you have is going to be used for testing, and then the model is going to be trained on k-1 folds. The process is going to be repeated K amount of times, and each time that you do this will have a different group of the data that you will use for validation.

a. There are a few advantages that come with this one. First, the computation time is going to be reduced as we go through the process 10 times, or less, depending on what value you give to k.

b. This one is also going to have a reduced bias so you can rely on the information that you have more.

c. Every point of data gets to be tested just once and is used in training the k-1 times.

d. The variance of the resulting estimate is going to be reduced the number of times that k increases.

e. There are some disadvantages of k fold or the 10-old cross-validation. The training algorithm, compared to some of the other options, is going to be computationally intensive because the algorithm has to start over again and rerun from scratch k times to be effective.

3. When we are done with this part, we are going to move on to the stratified cross-validation. This is going to be another technique that works well

because it is going to help us to arrange out the data so that each fold will be the right representation of the data set, and will force the process so that all of the folds are going to have the least m instance for each class. This approach is going to work well because it will make sure that the data is not going to be overrepresented, especially when the variable that we would like to focus on with our target is not balanced out well.

a. A good example of this is when we handle a problem of binary classification when we would like to predict whether or not someone who was on the Titanic was a survivor or not. We will then ensure that each of the folds that we have will include a percentage of the passengers who survived and a certain percentage of those who did not make it.

4. Another option that we are able to work with is known as the time-series cross-validation. This is where we see that splitting up our time series into a manner that is more random is not going to help us out as much. This is due to the fact that the time-related data is going to end up being messy. If we are working on figuring out the prices of the stocks that we want to work with, then we are able to split up the data in a random manner. This is why we

would want to work with cross-validation. With this one, each day is going to be part of our test data, and then we would need to consider the data that we worked with from the day before as some of our training set.

a. A good place to start with this one is by training out the model on the minimum amount of observations and then we will be able to focus on this data and using it for the next day to help us test the data. And then we will keep moving through the days like this in order to help the algorithm to learn ore. This is going to make it easier for us to consider the aspect of the time-series that will come up with this kind of prediction.

The Hyperparameter Optimization

The next thing that we need to take a closer look at when we are working with our optimization is the idea of the hyperparameters. These are going to be important because they are properties that are specific to the model that we want to work with, ones that will be fixed before we really have a chance to test or train the data that we have with this model. Before we spend too much time trying to get through all of this though, we have to take a look at some of the optimization of this that we talked about earlier, because this is going to make it easier for us to handle some of what we talk about here.

A good way to take a look at the idea of a hyperparameter optimization is to look at the random forest. This hyperparameter is going to help us out because it will tell us how many decision trees we are going to have in the random forest that you are working with. When we want to handle one of the neural networks, we will find that there is going to be a rate of learning, the layers that are going to be hidden, the number of units that you would like to show up in all of these layers, and even the types of parameters that we are focusing on as well.

While we are able to bring up the topic of tuning our hyperparameter, we are going to not look at something that is outside of searching for the hyperparameters that we are able to use to make sure we get the high accuracy and precision that we are looking for. When we are ready to optimize these parameters, we will end up with one of the hardest parts of the whole process that we need to handle here. But it is so important to helping us to get things done as well.

The main aim that we will get when using this is that we want to find the sweet spot along the way. This is going to be the sweet spot of the model and will be the most important because it allows us to get the best performance on the projects that we do possible. The neat thing with this one though is that we are able to find a few techniques that will make life easier for parameter tuning, but the two most important ones and the ones that we are going to spend our time on the most here will be the random search and the grid search.

Random and Grid Search

And the last thing that we are going to look at when we work with this chapter is how the grid search and the random search are going to work in comparison to one another. This is important because it helps a program to figure out which out of these two is going to be the best for the work and results that we want to see. Before we dive too much into this one, we have to review some of the hyperparameter optimizations and see how this is going to fit into this kind of section as well.

First, our goal is to learn more about a process that is known as grid searching. This is where we are going to go through and try out all of the combinations of a list that we have to those hyperparameters, and then we will be able to evaluate each of these combinations to see what will happen. The pattern that we then choose to work with here is going to be similar to what we are able to see on the grid from before, but this is because the values will be placed into a kind of matrix to sort them out.

When the matrix is being set, we will be able to set up all of our parameters so that we can look them over and take them into consideration, taking a note at how accurate each one is going to be. Once all of these can be evaluated on their own the model that has the most accurate parameters out of all our choices will be the right one that we want to work with.

There are going to be times when we will decide that it is best to work with the method known as the grid search. But while this is a good option to work with, sometimes it is going to be too complex and too long to work with. This is where we are going to switch our work over to a random search. This is going to be a good technique where some of the random combinations of the hyperparameter that we use to help us figure out the best solution for the model that we are able to build up.

There are going to be many cases when this search is going to help us to look through the information and can help us try out a few of the combinations that may seem random for the range of values that we have. To help us to optimize this kind of random search though, the function will need to go through an evaluation at some of the random configurations of the parameter space along with the other work.

The chances that we have of finding the parameter that is the most optimal for our needs are going to increase when we work with the random search. This is because the pattern is going to be rained on in the optimized parameters, and we will not need to know some of the aliases ahead of time. Then the random search is going to be able to work the best when we are working with some of the data that is considered lower-dimensional data because the time that will be taken to help us find the right set for this is going to be lower when you don't need to go through as many iterations to get it done.

We will find here that the random search is going to be one of the best techniques out of the two that we are able to work with, especially when the number of dimensions that we need to focus on is lower. There are a lot of concerns, both theoretical and practical, that we need to work with when we evaluate these strategies. And the strategy that ends up being the best for the particular problem that we are working with is going to always be the one that is able to find the best value that we can work with, without having to go through as many evaluations.

Keep in mind when we are going through with this one is that the grid search is sometimes seen as a machine learning algorithm that is less common. This is why we are more likely to work with the random search to get the work done. This random search is able to get us the same, and often better, values when we compare it over to the grid search, and we won't have to go through as many evaluations of the functions for some of the problems that we want to be able to work with as well. Of course, though, we need to decide which method is going to be the best for some of the work that we would like to do in the process as well.

Chapter 12: Other Algorithms That Work Well with Python Machine Learning

Before we are done with this guidebook and all that we are able to learn from it along the way, it is time for us to take a look at just a few more of the algorithms that we are able to use when it comes to Python and machine learning working together. You will find that there are endless amounts of machine learning algorithms that we are able to work with when it is time to handle data science or some of the other cool things that you are able to do with machine learning. And often you are only limited by what you would like to do with the information and any challenges that you may face along the way. With this in mind, some of the different algorithms that you are able to use, that we have not discussed in this guidebook yet, will include:

Naïve Bayes

The first option that we are going to spend some time on here is going to be the Naïve Bayes algorithm. To get a better understanding of how we are able to make sure that this one works, we will need to imagine something for a moment. Let's start out by pretending that we are doing some new project, and it comes with a few challenges of classification along the way. At the same time, we are looking at these challenges and we want to figure out which hypothesis is going to work out the best for this. Then there is the problem of figuring out a design that is good because you want to add in the right features and discussions based on how important all of the variables are to the model.

This is a lot of things that we need to try and balance about our project to make sure that it is going to work the way that we want, and it may seem like a tall order for just one of the algorithms that we have. But the Naïve Bayes is able to help us get it done. Once we have been able to go through and gather up the information that we need, you will also find that there will be shareholders in the company, or at least some important investors, who are interested in seeing a model of what you plan to do.

This may seem hard to do. All you have right now is the data and a little plan. But the shareholders and investors want to be able to go through and see what is going to happen and what they can expect, without waiting a long time for you to be able to get it all done to show them. And you want to make sure that you show that information in a manner that is easy to understand and doesn't use a ton of technical jargon along the way.

This is going to be a big dilemma for you as a programmer to start out with. First, when you are to this stage, the information that you are working with is not going to be done. And even if you had a better handle on the information here, you may think that it is too complex for another person to look at here. How are we able to make it all set up so that the investors can see what is going on, even though you are not done yet, but making one of these models isn't going to be easy, and you have to worry about how complete it as well, and that is a challenge that we have to learn how to handle.

Often, when we are working with the process of data analysis, you may end up with a model that has hundreds of thousands of points that you need to work with and show on the model. It is even possible that while you are doing some of the recommended training and testing that some new variables will show up that you have to consider as well. with all of this information going on around us and with us not being done with all of it, how are we able to really go through the information and then make sure it is in the format that is the easiest for us to understand along the way.

The good news with this one and the thing that we need to remember when we work with the Naïve Bayes is that it is one of the best algorithms to work with in order to help us really get through the beginning stages done and going. It is designed to help us to really present all of the different types of information that we need, while still making sure that it is simple enough that everyone is able to use, even those who are not data scientists will be able to understand what is going on and make sense of it all.

This model is a good one for the data scientist to put together as well. And since it is going to be used to help you get through some of the biggest sets of data in a way that is simplified, you will find that it is one of the best methods for us to use as well for this kind of situation. One of the advantages that we are going to see with this kind of model though is that it is simple, and that simplicity is going to make it one of the best options to use when you are getting started with some of the machine learning that you want to work with.

As you start to learn more about the Naïve Bayes algorithm, you may find that there are a ton of reasons why you would want to learn how to make this one work for some of your needs. For example, this is a good one to use because of its ease of use, and this is even more true for those who are beginners and who have never been able to work in machine learning or deep learning in the past.

You will then find that the Naïve Bayes algorithm is going to be an effective method to work with when it is time for us to make some predictions for the sets of data that we are using and which classes they should end up in. This is a good thing because it helps to keep things in the set of data as simple as possible. It does have a high-performance level though too, despite being one of the easier algorithms to learn, and it can often seem more sophisticated to work with than it may be.

While there are going to be a number of benefits that we are able to work with when it comes to handling the Naïve Bayes model, it is important to know that there are a few negatives as well, just like with any of the other algorithms that we can spend our time on. The first downfall of this algorithm is that when you work with an algorithm that is going to be set with categorical variables, you have to make sure that the data you are going through for the testing phase is not the same data that you used for training. This will then cause you to end up with predictions that are not that accurate, and then you have to rely on probability, which is not all that accurate either.

Markov Algorithm

Another option that we are able to take some time looking over is going to be known as the Markov algorithm. This one is going to fit under the umbrella of the unsupervised machine learning that we will want to do on some of our projects. This is a good algorithm for us to work with because it is going to help us gather up all of the data that we choose to place into it, and then it will translate it out so that it can work with the coding language of our choice. This may work with Python if that is the coding language that you want to focus on, but it is also going to work with other coding languages as well.

One of the reasons that a lot of programmers like to work with this algorithm is because it allows them to choose some of the rules that they are able to use ahead of time with this algorithm so that it takes on the direction that they wish. Many programmers like the Markov Algorithm because it helps them to come up with the rules, rather than them having to always follow the rules and trying to make the data fit into this. You can use this benefit in order to take a whole string of data and make sure that it is something useful for the job or the project that you are handling at the time.

The second thing that programmers often like with this kind of algorithm is that there are several methods that work with this one, rather than just one path. One option to consider here is that the algorithm is going to be something that a lot of programmers can use on projects like FNA. For example, you could use this algorithm on a sequence of DNA, and then use it to translate some of the information that is found inside of all that.

This is going to help us make things easier for a lot of o people including scientists, doctors, and programmers so that they can see what information is inside of the DNA and then make better predictions in the future as well. when you are working with a computer as a programmer, you will find that the DNA sequence is sometimes hard to go through and understand all that well, but it is often easier to look through and understand the numerical data, and this is where the Markov Algorithm is able to help.

You may also find that another reason to work with the Markov algorithm is that it is going to be good when you would like to learn about problems where you can put in the right input but you are a bit uncertain about the parameters. This algorithm is going to be able to find the insights that are inside of that information. There are some situations where these insights are going to be hidden, and it is going to be able to find some of these insights better than other algorithms can do in some situations.

Of course, while there are a lot of benefits that come with using this algorithm, there are also going to be some times when it may not be the best algorithm for your needs either. To start, the Markov algorithm is going to be a bit more difficult to work with compared to some of the other options out there. This is because you have to manually do the work any time you would like to create a new rule so that a second or third programming language can be used along with this algorithm.

If you only plan to use this algorithm with the Python language and never bring in another coding language along the way, then this is going to be something that you will not need to work with. But often your coding and the work that you want to do with machine learning will need more than one programming language to get it done, and if you end up needing to rewrite out the rules that you want in your codes a bunch of times, the process is going to get tedious.

Regression Algorithms

While you will find that there are many times when you can work with the Naïve Bayes algorithm to get your work done, there are times when it will not quite do the trick, and you may need to rely on something like the regression analysis. This is going to be the algorithm type that you will want to spend your time on if you are trying to see what relationship, if any, is there between the dependent variables and the predictor.

Programmers are going to be able to quickly find out that this is a technique that works well for them and they can use it in many situations where they need to be able to see if there is some kind of causal relationship between the forecasting that they see, with the various variables that they plan to work with, or even if they are working on the time series modeling that is in place.

The whole point of choosing this type of algorithm over some of the others is that it is going to be a good one to help you grab all of the information out of your data set and then get it to work, as closely as possible to one line or curve. Of course, depending on the data that you plan to use here, this line may not have as many points on it as you would like. But it is a good place for us to start, in a more visual form, to see if there are some similarities in the data that we are working with.

There are times when a company or a data scientist is going to choose to handle this kind of algorithm because it is a good one when we want to make predictions. The company will then take the predictions that come out of these regression algorithms in order to increase their profits overall in some manner. It is even possible to work with this kind of algorithm to make an estimate of how much the sales of a company can grow, while still having the ability to base it on how the economy and the conditions of this are doing at the time.

There are a lot of things that we are able to enjoy when it comes to the regression algorithm, but one thing that a lot of data scientists like with this one is that it has room for them to add in some of the pertinent information that they would like to use. You are able to go through and add in any information that you want if you think that it will help you to get a more accurate prediction as well. so, adding in information about how the economy is doing now, and how it was doing in the past, could be important and useful based on the data that you want to handle as well.

This is important here is that the regression algorithm is going to be used to help us figure out the most likely and the most profitable way that we will see some growth in our company in the future. But to make sure that this one works the way that we would need, we have to make sure that the company is putting in the right kind of data and information, or the predictions could come out wrong.

One example that we are able to see with this is if the company is trying to find the right algorithm of machine learning so that they can learn not just if their company is growing, but to see what rate the company is growing and if this is similar, faster, or slower compared to some of the other companies that they compete against. We can then use this information to make some predictions on how the company will do in the future and then they can make some changes if this is not up to their standards.

We will find that there is more than one algorithm that can be considered in the term regression, and you have to really know about your data and what you would like to accomplish with it, in order to figure out which of these algorithms is the best for you to choose. While there are a number of options that work well, some of the most common of these regression algorithms that your company may be able to benefit from includes:

1. Stepwise regression
2. Linear regression
3. Logistic regression
4. Polynomial regression
5. Ridge regression

As you can see here, working with the regression algorithm will be able to present us with a few different kinds of benefits if you choose to use it. To start out with, you will see that these are the algorithms that can make it easier for anyone using the information to check whether there is some kind of relationship present to work with at all, between the dependent and independent variables. This is also the algorithm to use in order to show what kind of impact is going to show up if you try to add in a new variable or change up to another kind of variable that is in the set of data if you want to experiment with what is there a bit.

We also have to look at some of the downsides that come with this method to get a full picture of what is there. There are a few issues that come up, and one of the biggest of these is that you will notice how the regression algorithms, due to their name, will not be able to help you out with the classification problems that you have. The reason that these two ideas do not work out is that the regression algorithm is more likely to overfit the data in many situations. So if you try to add in a lot of different constraints here, you will find that it doesn't take long before the process gets tedious and you can often find a better algorithm in order to help handle this kind of thing instead.

Q-Learning

Now it is time for us to end with a look at how we are able to do something with the reinforcement learning that we talked about earlier. There are a lot of times when we will want to work with that kind of machine learning, but you will find that some of the algorithms really are not as glamorous or well-known as we are used to seeing with some of the other options along the way. That is going to change here when we take a look at what we are able to do with this kind of learning algorithm.

With the Q-learning algorithm, we are going to work with any kind of project that wants to focus on something known as temporal difference learning. As we are working with machine learning, you will notice that this algorithm is more of an off-policy option. It is known in this manner because it is not going to have the ability to learn the action-value function in a manner similar to the other options of algorithms. Sometimes this is a good thing, and other times it could add some issues to the learning that you would like to work with.

Since this is going to be a useful option to a programmer because they are able to use it no matter the function they would like to create in the data set, it is still important for us to go through and learn a bit more about this method and what it is able to do for us. The learner needs to do this ahead of time because it is going to help them to pick out the course of action that is the best for them. Of course, keep in mind with this one that one of the drawbacks to using it is that it has a few more steps to get the model done compared to some of the other steps. But because it is going to be more efficient than the other models, and because it does work well, you may find that the time and the effort are well worth it in the long run.

After you have been able to go through with this algorithm and find the action-value function that will work the best for your data points, it is time for you to create what is going to be known as the optimal policy. How are we supposed to be able to construct this with the Q-learning algorithm? The best way to get started with this is to use the actions that you think will come in at the highest value, regardless of the state that has been chosen to do this one in.

Depending on the kind of data that you want to go through, and the results that you are hoping to get, there could be a number of great advantages that come with using the algorithm in machine learning for Q-learning. One of the benefits of this is that you won't have to go through all of the effort or the time that is needed to put in the models of the environment so that the system is able to compare the means. You will be able to compare a few, and often a lot, of actions together and compare how they are going to be together. In addition, you can use any kind of environment that you would like to with this one, and still get the same results and be able to make the predictions that you would like.

You will find though that there are a few negatives that are likely when we work with this kind of reinforcement learning. We have to focus on how the main issue is that we will have to take on more steps to ensure this learning is going to happen. This process, because you do need to go through and write out the rules that you want to use and the course of action that will make the most sense to reach your goals, will provide us with more steps compared to a few of the other options. For those programmers who are in a hurry to be done, and who don't really care as much about the rules they put in place, this may not be the best option to choose.

As we can see from this kind of machine learning algorithm, and some of the many others that we have been able to explore in this guidebook, there are a lot of options when it is time to work with machine learning and getting the data sorted through and understandable in no time. There is no right or wrong algorithm that we are able to choose from. It is more about making sure that we go with the option that is right for our situation. This changes based on the situation, the data we have, the solution that we want, and so much more, but learning what this is and how we are able to use it to our advantage is going to help as well. All of these algorithms are great, and it is more about finding the one that is right for us, rather than choosing the one that is right or wrong all of the time.

Conclusion

Thank you for making it through to the end of *Learn Python*. Let's hope it was informative and able to provide you with all of the tools you need to achieve your goals whatever they may be.

The next step is to spend some time learning more about some of these amazing options in algorithms and more that you are able to focus on when it comes to handling machine learning and the Python language. When it comes to using Python and finally being able to really learn about the data that you have, and all of the different benefits that come with data science, you will find that this is the exciting part of the process. It is the part where we can actually take all of the data that we have and put it through the algorithm, finally getting the insights and the predictions that we are looking for.

And this is where we are going to spend some of our time exploring this guidebook as well. This guidebook is going to spend most of its time taking a look at some of the best algorithms that you are able to use when it comes to working on machine learning, especially when it comes to Python, and this can help you to really figure out which one is going to be the best for your own work with the data. You may be surprised by how many options there are when it comes to algorithms though, which is why we are going to spend some of our time looking through them and going through them in more detail.

In addition to learning about the benefits of working with Python and why this is often the most chosen out of all the languages when it is time to handle machine learning and some of its various algorithms for data science, we are going to really take a closer look at some of the great algorithms that we would want to use in this situation. Whether you are looking to create an algorithm that is for supervised, unsupervised, or reinforcement learning, we spent some time talking about how to use each one, when they are all going to be beneficial for your needs, and so much more.

Working with machine learning is a really great experience. There are going to be so many times when we are able to bring this up, and each industry, no matter what they work with or how they serve the customer, will be able to enjoy some of the benefits of machine learning. The more that it is used in our modern world, the more that we will be able to discover it and use it in the future. This is something that can be really exciting when it is time to work with machine learning. The algorithms that we are going to explore inside will help us to utilize this to its full potential.

There are so many times when we will want to work with machine learning, Python, and some of the machine learning algorithms that are explored in this guidebook. When we are ready to start learning more about these topics and how we are able to work with this process, or even if you are ready to use it for some of your own data science needs, make sure to check out this guidebook to see the steps that are needed to get started.

Finally, if you found this book useful in any way, a review on Amazon is always appreciated!

Python Data Science

Learn the Ethics of Coding in a
Day by Taking My Classes

TIM WIRED

Introduction

Congratulations on purchasing *Python Data Science* and thank you for doing so.

The following chapters are going to give us a more in-depth look at what we need in order to get things done when it is time to handle any project with data science. Many companies are jumping on board when it is time to work with data science and all that it can provide to us in terms of beating out the competition, learning more about the competition, and so much more. There isn't a single industry out there that is not able to benefit from working with a data science look at themselves, and this guidebook is going to spend some time exploring this in more depth to help us get started.

At the beginning of this guidebook, we are going to spend some time exploring more about data science and what we are able to do with it to help us reach our goals. We will also take a look at some of the benefits of working with this process, and how it can all come together when we add in the Python language to the mix as well.

From there it is time to spend more of our energy on some of the different steps that we need to use in order to make data science success for our needs. For example, we will spend some time taking a look at some of the libraries that are available through Python that can really get the work done for you, look at some of the steps that come with organizing and cleaning your data before using it, and even why it is so important to gather the right kinds and amounts of data to get some of the results that you would like.

There are just so many parts that come into the data science project, and simply set it all up so that the information is ready to go after your analysis. If the data is not gathered, and you are not able to clean up and handle some of the outliers that are there, then you will find that it is really hard to go through and actually get the accurate results that you need from a data science project.

Once we have all of that done, it is time to get into the importance of data analysis. Not only will we take a look at some of the steps that you need to use in order to get started with this process of data analysis, but we will look at how machine learning is able to fit into this process and help us to get so much done in the process. Machine learning, along with the variety of methods and algorithms that go with it, will be so important when it is time to work on any data science project, and will help us to finally take all of that data that we have been working with so far, and expand it so that we are able to really get some good results and know how to use it.

This is not the end of our exploration when we go through this process though. We are also going to spend some time taking a look at data science from the view of why visuals are so important to understanding the data that we have and some of the best visuals that we are able to use to get the results that we want. We can also end this with a look at some of the benefits of working with this process and how data science, when it is used properly, is going to be able to help us to finally get some of the results that we want in the present, and in the future.

There are so many businesses that are going to benefit when it comes to working with data analysis and seeing this work for some of their needs. It is always a good idea to learn a bit more about this process and how you are able to really use it to learn more about your customers, learn how to beat out your competition, and so much more. But we have to learn that there are a lot of steps that come into play, and we can't just skip right to the predictions and insights, no matter how much we would like to do this.

Data science is going to be a process that has a lot of different parts that come together with each other, and when we learn how to make these work, we are going to see some amazing results in the process as well. It is really as simple as all of that! When you follow the steps of gathering the right data, organizing and cleaning your data, data mining, a data analysis, and even adding in some visuals of the data, in the end, you will find that there is so much more than you are able to do with this process overall.

When you are ready to learn about data science and how you are able to benefit from this process you have to go through a number of steps to make this happen. It may seem like a lot of work, but the goal of this guidebook is to help you get started and to ensure that you are ready to take on some of the work that you need along the way. When your business is ready to use this and see some of the great benefits that come with it, make sure to read through this guidebook to help you get started.

There are plenty of books on this subject on the market, thanks again for choosing this one! Every effort was made to ensure it is full of as much useful information as possible, please enjoy it!

Chapter 1: The Basics of Data Science

Looking at the world around us, we have entered the era of big data, the need for its storage is also going to grow. It was one of the biggest challenges that a lot of industries were facing in the past, at least until 2010. The main focus of that time was a bit different at that time compared to what we are doing now, which is to build up a framework and find other solutions that would help to store the data that we have.

Today, there are a lot of options out there that we are able to use when it is time to store the data that we need. And because of this, some of the focus on data has switched over to how we are going to process this data. Data science is the key that we need to focus on when it is time to work with this. All of the ideas that you see in our favorite sci-fi movies can actually turn into reality when we are able to work with the process of data science in the proper manner. Often, we will find that data science is going to be one of the future parts of artificial intelligence. This is part of why data science is so important for us to understand and we need to see how it is able to add in some more value to our business.

With some of this in mind, we need to take a look at what data science is all about and how we are able to make this work for some of our needs. There are a lot of parts that are going to come into play when we are working with data science and learning more about how it works is going to make all of the difference.

Why Does My Business Need Data Science?

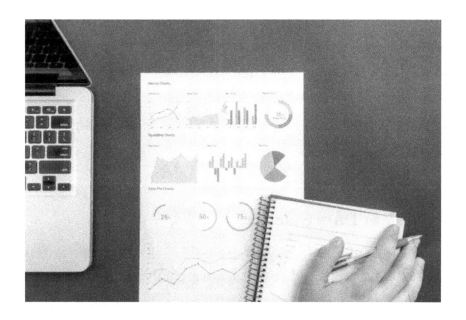

In a traditional sense, the data that we had was going to be small and structured in size. This is going to make it easier to work with and allows us to get all of this done with some of the simple business intelligence tools that we need. But unlike the data that we are used to seeing in a traditional system, most of the data that we are going to find today is going to be either semi-structured or unstructured. This makes it a bit more complicated to work with and can cause us to need to accomplish a bit more work in order to see it happen as well.

The data that we are going to work with today, this data is going to come to us in a lot of different sources like text files, multimedia forms, financial logs, and sensors to name a few. And because there are so many sources and more, and that the data is more complicated than before, we will find that the basic business intelligence tools that were used in the past are not able to handle all of the data. This led to the need for more complex and advanced tools to help us to process and analyze the data in the hopes of getting some of the insights and patterns out of the process.

A Look at Data Science

From here, we need to spend some time taking a look at data science even more and see what we are able to do to make this work for our needs. The use of the term data science is going to creep up in a lot of the different things that you are going to try and do with your business. And it is likely that you have heard a lot about this option from your friends and other business partners. But it is important to know exactly what this all means and why it is so important before we dive in.

For example, it is a good idea to have certain skills ahead of time to turn into data scientists. You may want to know what some of the differences are between these data science processes and business intelligence in the past. And then we may want to know how some of the predictions and decisions are going to be made in data science in the first place.

These are just a few of the questions that we are going to have when it is time to work with data science, but first, we need to take a look at some of the different things that we need to take a look at when it comes to data science. To start with, data science is going to be a blend of a lot of different principles of machine learning, algorithms, and tools that all come together to help us discover what patterns and insights are going to be found in the raw data that we are working with.

For the most part, a data analyst is going to be someone who is going to explain what is going on by processing the history of all the data that we have. on the other hand, we will find that a data scientist is not only going to do the exploratory analysis to help us discover some of the insights that are in it, but it will also use some of the algorithms of machine learning that are more advanced, and some of the basic ones, to help us o identify the occurrence of a particular event in the future. But you will find that the data scientist will look at the data from a lot of different angles, and sometimes these angles will not be ones that are known earlier.

So, for the most part, you will find that data science is going to be used in most cases to help us make predictions and decisions. There are a few options that we are able to work with to make this happen and these include options like machine learning, prescriptive analytics, and predictive causal analytics. Let's take a look at how we are able to work with all of these and how we can make sure that they give us the results that we need.

The first option is going to be predictive causal analytics. If you would like to work with a model that is good at making predictions of what is going to happen in the future, you need to apply this kind of analytics along the way. So, if your business is going to provide money on credit, then the probability of a customer making their credit payments in the future on time is a matter of concern for you. You want to make sure that you will actually earn the payments that you deserve, rather than handing over the money and never seeing it again.

With the predictive causal analytics, you will be able to build a model that is able to perform these analytics on how well the customer has paid their bills in the past, and how well they will be able to make the payments in the future. If the numbers look good, then you will be able to give them the money with a good degree of certainty in order to get started with this process and will loan them money.

Then you are able to work with what is known as prescriptive analytics. If you are looking to work with a model that has the intelligence of taking on its own decisions, and the ability to help modify it with the dynamic parameters, you will need to work with this kind of analytics for it to get this done. This is going to be a relatively new field is all about providing advice. In some other terms, it is going to come in to make a prediction but will suggest a range of the actions and outcomes that are associated with it.

The third option that we are able to work with is going to be machine learning. We can use this in a few different manners, such as making predictions. If you are working on something like the transactional data for a financial company, and you are hoping to build up a model to help determine the future trend, then machine learning algorithms are going to be one of the best bets. This is going to fall under the idea of supervised learning. This is because supervised because you can hold onto the data based on which you can train the machines. For example, you can train up a fraud detection model that can be trained with the help of a historical record of fraudulent purchases to help keep you safe.

There is another method that we are able to work with when it comes to machine learning, and this is going to be to help us with some pattern discovery. If you do not already have some parameters that you would like to use to help base your predictions, then it is important to take some time to find the patterns that are hidden inside of the set of data that you have in order to make the predictions that will move your business forward.

This one, in particular, is going to be more of an unsupervised model because you are not going to have any kind of labels ahead of time for the grouping. There are a number of these algorithms that we are able to work with here, but one of the most common options that will help us with some pattern discovery is going to be known as clustering.

Data Science and Business Intelligence

If your business has been working with data for some time, it is likely that you have spent some time working with business intelligence at least a little bit. These ideas are going to sound like they are similar, but we are going to take a look at how these are going to have some parts that are a little bit different, and why this is going to be so important for your work.

The first thing that we need to take a look at is going to be known as business intelligence, or BI. It is going to help us to analyze the data that we already have in order to find some hindsight and insight to describe the trends in the business. This one is going to help us to take data from both internal and external sources, prepare it the right way, run queries on it, and then create a nice dashboard to answer the questions that you have. You could work with things like business problems or work on a quarterly revenue analysis on this one for example. It is also helpful when it is time to evaluate the impact of certain events in the near future.

Then we are able to work with data science. This one is going to be an approach that looks more towards the future compared to BI. This one is going to spend more time exploring things with the focus on analyzing the past or the current data and then using this to help us predict the outcomes that are going to happen in the future. And the main point of working with this is to help us to make some informed decisions in the future. It is a good way for us to learn how to answer the how and the what of the events that are occurring around us.

One of the common mistakes that are often made when it comes to working on projects in data science is that they rush through data collection and analysis, without understanding the requirements, or even having their business problem framed in the proper manner. this is why it is important for us to be able to go through the proper steps, or the lifecycle of data science, to make sure that the project is going to run in the smooth manner that we would like along the way.

The Lifecycle of Data Science

While we are going through this process, we have to remember that there is actually a type of lifecycle that we need to work with. All of these steps are going to be important to some of the work that we are trying to do along the way and missing out on any of them is going to be a bad idea when you want to get the right predictions and insights out of that data. We are going to take a closer look at some of these later on, but you will find that data science has a number of steps that are going to be important when it is time for us to learn the real patterns and insights that are inside of all that data.

The first step in this lifecycle that we need to take a look at is the discovery phase. Before you get started with the project, it is important to understand some of the things that you would like to see happen. It is important to know the specifications, priorities, requirements, and even the budget that you need to be able to stick with during this project.

You also need to have a good ability to go through and ask the right questions through all of this. Here, you are going to assess if you have the right resources present for your work in terms of having the right kinds of people who can gather and analyze the data, the technology that can get this done, the right amount of time to take on this kind of project, and even the right kind of data to help support the project that we need to get it all done.

During this phase, we also need to spend some time framing what our business problem is all about so that we can get it all done. If we have no idea what our business process is all about, and what problem we want to be able to solve, then with all of the data that is there, we are going to end up with a big mess and will spend way time and energy when it is time to look through that data. And this can help us to formulate some of the hypotheses that we would like to get started and to help us test things out as we go through it.

Then we move on to the data preparation part of this process. In this kind of phase, we are going to need to work with what is known as an analytical sandbox to help us get the analytics that we would like done for the entirety of the project that we are doing. This is going to make it easier for us to go through and explore some of the different parts that are present in our work and will ensure that we are going to really get a chance to learn about the data that is there.

During this phase, we need to spend some time learning more about the data. This means that we need to work on exploring, preprocessing, ETLT, and to help us get data into the sandbox that we are working with. This is all-important to ensure that we are set up with and will ensure that we are going to really get set up here.

But before we are able to put the data through the model that we are hoping to use, later on, you will find that the best step that we have to take is to go through the data and really prepare it. If there are missing values, duplicate values, or it is not in the right format, then you are going to end up in trouble and the algorithm is either not going to offer you any kind of results, or the results that you get will not be as accurate as you would like.

There are a few languages that you are able to use when it is time to clean, transform, and visualize the data that you are working with. You will find that this will work well if you focus on the R or the Python language. This is going to be a good step where we get to spend time on outliers in the data and will help us to establish the relationship that we need between the variables that we have. once you have been able to clean up and then prepare the data, it is then time to move through and do what is known as exploratory analytics on it to get the best results.

The third step that we are able to work with is going to be known as model planning. In this one, we are going to spend some time determining which techniques and methods we would like to use in order to draw up the relationships that we need with variables. These relationships are going to set the base for all of the algorithms that you would like to implement in the phases that we will get to later.

For this step, we need to spend some time applying the EDA, or working with Exploratory Data Analytics with the help of a lot of different statistical formulas and visualization tools. There are a lot of options that you are able to work with when it is time to bring out the model planning tools, and some of the options that you are able to work with will include things like the right coding language, the SQL analysis services, and even the use of SAS and ACCESS.

Although there are many tools that are on the market for you to work with, you will find that the Python language is going to really work well for helping you to get through all of the processes that we are going through. You need to make sure though that you are able to spend some time planning out the model that you would like to use in order to get all of this done at the right time. There is the possibility that you will come up with more than one option when it is time to prepare a model, but we need to learn more about these and figuring out how we are able to work with each one, so that we can pick up the model and the algorithm in order to get the results that we want in the end.

From this point, we need to spend some time looking at the process of model building. When we are on this kind of phase, we are going to spend some time developing the sets of data that we would like to work with training and testing purposes. We can't just grab a model and assume that it is going to work that we would like to see. The results will not be accurate because the model as of yet, has no idea what you are hoping to see in the process.

Instead, you need to spend some time looking at the process that is necessary in order to really train the data that you would like through the model. This will ensure that it knows what you should work with, and over time, we will find that this is going to work better than ever before. But the right sets of data for training and testing will be necessary before you can rely on the patterns and insights that you will need.

During this phase, we really need to consider whether the tools that we already have will be enough to run the models that we have, or if we would need to bring in some more of a robust environment. You will analyze a lot of the different learning techniques that are needed in machine learning in order to help clustering, association, and classification to help up the model building that we would like to do.

The fifth step that we are going to focus on is going to be known as the operationalization. When we get to this phase, you are able to deliver some of the different parts that we need to explain what you were able to find in all of the models and algorithms that you have run that data through in the previous step. This one is going to include providing the people in the business who make big decisions information through technical documents, reports, code, and briefings.

In addition, you will find that in this step, it is possible to take some of the information that we have collected and used it in a type of pilot project that is done in real-time. This will usually only take place in a small part of the business, such as one of the offices, in order to see how it will work and whether it is the right option for you. If it works, then it can be expanded out to other parts of the company. But if it ends up not working, then there isn't as much waste in time or money to make this happen.

The pilot project is going to be important because it is going to really help us to see how the information that comes from the data that you collected is going to work, and whether it is the right decision for your business, without as much risk. It is a great way to get a clear picture of the performance and some of the other constraints that are related here on a small scale before we go through and work with a full deployment.

And finally, we are going to end with some communication of the results that we have. When we get to this point, we are going to find that it is important to evaluate whether or not we have really been able to achieve the goals that we planned out in the first phase. So, with this kind of phase, we are going to start by taking all of the key findings that we had in all of the other steps, and then organize it in a manner that will make it easier to understand.

This is often going to be done with the help of reports, spreadsheets, and other visuals that will help others who may not have the added technical experience in order to understand what is going on in the long run either. The data scientist has to go through and really go through this information and make sure that they are presenting it in a manner that the decision maker's in the company will understand. The methods that they will use depend on who they are working with.

So, once you have all of these key findings in place, you will need to communicate the information to the right places and then determine if the results of any pilot projects that you do will be a failure or a success based on the different parts and criteria that you were able to develop at the beginning of this project.

There are s many times when we are able to work with the data analysis and we will be able to see what data science is able to do for our business. But we have to make sure that we are going through and writing it out in the right manner, and that we use the right methods and models in order to get it done. We will explore through more of this as we go through this guidebook, but you will find that these steps above will help us to get more done in the process as well.

Chapter 2: How Does the Python Language Fit In With Data Science?

Now that we have spent some time taking a look at what data science is all about, it is time to bring in the work that we are able to do when it comes to the Python language. When we work with these models and all that can come up with data science, you will find that we need to write out some algorithms. We will take a look at machine learning later on, but Python will work well with machine learning and can help us to write up and execute the algorithms that we want to create in this process as well. We could go with some of the other languages that are out there, but Python is often one of the best options to use.

The Python language is going to be one of the best options to work with when it is time to work with any of the projects in data science that we would like to accomplish. there are actually going to be a lot of projects that you are able to do with these ideas of data science, and Python is able to help us to get more of it done in the process. There are also a lot of other reasons that you would want to work with the Python language in order to make sure that you get your projects done.

This language, even though you are going to find that there are a number of complexities that are able to come with it as well, is going to be really easy for a beginner to learn more about. If you are someone who is just getting started with coding to help you finish the algorithms that we have in this, and you are a bit worried about getting started, you may find that Python is going to be the best one to work choose from. Python is designed for the beginner to work with, and even if you have never done anything with the coding of any sort in the past, Python will make the process as simple and painless as possible.

One of the main points of choosing Python for some of your coding needs is that it makes sure that your coding is as simple and easy as possible, whether you are a professional coder or someone just starting out. The words that are used in this are

English, the syntax is simple, and it relies on the idea of being an object-oriented programming language. This means that it is easy and powerful and will meet your needs when it comes to finishing up a data science kind of project.

There is still a lot of power that comes with the Python language, even though it is designed for a beginner to learn to code for the first time. Many people worry that when they get started with the Python language that it is going to be too simplistic. They may reason that because this kind of language is designed to help beginners get started with their work, it is going to be too simple in order to get any of the more complex codes done and ready to go.

This can't be further from the truth. You will find that working with Python is a great option, even with the ease of use, that is strong enough to handle some of the more complex codes and projects that you would like to get done. For example, Python is able to help out, with the right libraries and extensions, things like machine learning, deep learning, science, mathematics, and other complicated processes, whether they are needed for data science or not.

More productivity for the programmer: The Python language has a lot of designs that are object-oriented and a lot of support libraries. Because of all these resources and how easy it is to use the program, the programmer is going to increase their productivity. This can even be used to help improve the productivity of the programmer while using languages like C#, C++, C, Perl, VB, and even Java.

When it is time for you to work on some of the different parts of your data science project, having more of that productivity is going to be so important overall. You will find that when the programmer is able to get more things done in a shorter amount of time, it ensures that they are going to see a big difference in the project they are working with.

Integration features: Python can be great because it integrates what is known as the Enterprise Application Integration. This really helps with a lot of the different things you want to work on in Python including COBRA, COM, and more. It also has some powerful control capabilities as it calls directly through Java, C++, and C. Python also has the ability to process XML and other markup languages because it can run all of the modern operating systems, including Windows, Mac OS X, and Linux through the same kind of byte code.

While we have spent most of our time right now focusing mainly on how we are able to work with Python in order to make sure we finish up any of the projects that we want in data science, there are going to be a few data science libraries that we have to add in with Python to gain the kind of compatibility that we need and to make sure that we are able to properly handle our algorithms and get the work done.

But this is part of why working with Python here is going to be so amazing. Python is compatible with many language options, which means that you can use a lot of the libraries and extensions that you want for a project, while still getting some of the ease of use that you will need from Python.

Another benefit that we are able to focus on here is that Python has a very large community. For someone who is just getting started with coding, having a nice big community to answer your questions, to help show you the best way to get started, and more will really be helpful. Data science and some of the algorithms that are needed for it are going to really need some complex coding, and Python is going to have a nice community to help you out with this.

The community that is available with Python comes from all parts of the world, and you will find programmers of all different coding levels. They can offer you some advice, give you some of the codes that you need, and will make it easier to get through some of the issues that you may face when it comes to some of the algorithms that you have in data science.

The next benefit on the list that we get to enjoy is some of the standard libraries of Python. This library is going to come with a lot of power to make sure that your coding tasks get all done. When you download this language at the start, you will find that this library is going to come with it, and will already be able to handle a lot of the functions, methods, and codes that you would like to do right from the beginning.

Keep in mind though that while the standard library of Python is going to be powerful and provide you with lots of options, when it comes to working with data science, there are going to be times when you need to add on some extensions to help make sure that you can get machine learning and more done. But there are a lot of choices when it comes to these, and learning how to make them work will make a difference in some of the coding that you would like.

Simply by working with the standard Python library that comes with your installation, there are a lot of powerful types of codes that you are able to write out including conditional statements, inheritances, and loops. All of these are things that you are able to use, and even though they are basics of learning to code, they will help out with some of the algorithms that we want to use later on.

There are a lot of special extensions and libraries that we are able to do with Python that is perfect for data science and machine learning. Even though there is a lot that we are able to do when it comes to using the Python language to help out just with the standard library, there are also a number of libraries that work not only with Python, but also help us to get more done with data science at the same time.

We are going to take some time to look at a lot of the different libraries for data science and Python, and you will get a chance to see how well these can help out with some of your data science projects. Some of the best options though, based on which machine learning algorithms you want to work with, include TensorFlow, Scikit-Learn, NumPy, SciPy, and Pandas.

Python is one of the options that is used to help out with creating the machine learning algorithms that you need to create your own models with data science. Without these models, you are going to end up having trouble going through all of that data you have been able to collect and actually find the insights and predictions that you want from that data. There are other languages you can use, most notably the R programming language, but Python is one of the best to help get all of this done.

There are also going to be a few steps that we are able to focus on when it is time to work with the projects that we need in data science. But one of these parts, the analysis part, we will have to work with a number of techniques including machine learning and deep learning. These help us to create a model that is needed in order to handle the large data that we want to work with. Going through all of this data is something that is pretty much impossible when you work on it in a manual manner. but with the right model that is run by the Python language, you will find that it is easy enough to sort through all of that information and get the predictions and insights that you are looking for out of the data in no time at all.

And this is really one of the main reasons that people will choose to work with the process of data science in the first place. The companies that decide to go with this because it allows them to take a large amount of raw data, and then figure out the insights that are found inside of that data. The models that are created in order to get this done, thanks the Python language and machine learning, can really make it easier for us to meet these goals and will make it easier to get ahead of the competition, meet the needs of the customers and the industry, and so much more.

There are going to be a ton of reasons why a data scientist is going to work with the process of this analysis with the help of the Python language. There are options in other coding languages that we are able to use, but you will quickly see that the Python language is going to be one of the best options that we can focus on to get the models created that we want, to work with the right kinds of libraries that we want with the use of machine learning and the right algorithms, and so much more.

Chapter 3: The Best Python Libraries to Help with Data Science

While we are on this topic of how well Python is able to work with data science, it is time to take a look at some of the different libraries that you are able to add onto Python and use when you would like to make sure that this language is going to work with some of the projects that you would like to accomplish with the data science project that you have in mind.

Remember that we talked a bit before how the standard library that comes with Python and how it is going to help us to learn a lot of the coding that we need and get things done in no time. however, we will find that a few of the models and algorithms that we want to do with data science are going to need a little bit more when it is time to work with your projects rather than the standard library.

The good news here is that we are able to work with some of the different libraries that are out there in order to help us get this done. And Python is going to have quite a few libraries and extensions that we are able to work with that can handle or data science projects and the other models and algorithms that we want to be able to work with overall. We just need to make sure that we go through and pick out the one that is going to work for the specific model or algorithm that you have in mind in the first place.

All of the libraries that you want to work with here are going to be a bit different and will handle some of the work that you want to do in a different manner. some of them are best for helping with the analysis and some may be better for handling some of the data gatherings that you want to do. This is why we need to learn a bit more about some of the libraries and what they will do for our needs.

These libraries are so important when it comes to some of the work that you want to do with algorithms and models. Without these libraries, you will not be able to complete some of the necessary tasks that come with data science, and it is going to really make it almost impossible to work with the predictions and insights that we need out of all there.

There are quite a few libraries that not only work with the Python language but will work with machine learning, data science, deep learning, and so much more. Some of the different libraries that you are able to pick from to get all of this done will include the following:

NumPy

When we first get started with doing some data science on Python, one of the best libraries to download is going to be NumPy. Many of the other data science libraries are going to rely on some of the capabilities that come with this kind of library, so having it set up and ready to go on your computer is going to make a big difference.

When you are ready to start working with some of the scientific tasks with Python, you are going to need to work with the Python SciPy Stack. This is going to be a collection of software that is specifically designed to help us complete some of the scientific computing that we need to do with Python. Keep in mind that this SciPy stack is not going to be the same thing as the SciPy library though so keep the two of these apart. The stack is going to be pretty big because there are more than 12 libraries that are found inside of it, and we want to put a focal point on the core package, particularly the most essential ones that help with data science.

The most fundamental package around which this computation stack is going to be built around is NumPy, which is going to stand for Numerical Python. It is going to provide us with an abundance of useful features for operations that you want to handle with matrices and n-arrays. This library is going to help us with a lot of different tasks that we want to do, including the vectorization of mathematical operations on the NumPy array type, which is going to ameliorate the performance and will speed up the execution that we see at the same time.

SciPy

Another library that we are able to take a look at when it comes to working with the Python language is going to be SciPy. This is going to be a library of software that we can use to help us handle some of the tasks that we need for engineering and science. If this is something that your project is going to need to spend some time on, then SciPy is the best library to get it done. You will quickly find that this library is going to contain some of the different modules that we need in order to help out with optimization, integration, statistics, and even some linear algebra if we would like to name a few of the different tasks that work well with this.

The main thing that we will use with this library and some of the functionality that you will need when bringing it up is that it is something we can build up with the help of the NumPy library from before. This means that the arrays that we want to use in SciPy are provided to us thanks to the NumPy library.

This library is going to provide us with some of the most efficient numerical routines as well as some of the numerical integrations that we need, the help of optimization, and a lot of the other options that we need with our specific submodules. The functions that are going to be discussed in this library are going to be documented as well to make it easier.

Pandas

We can't go far in our discussion over the libraries in Python that work with data analysis without spending some time looking at the Pandas library. This one is going to be designed to help us out with all of the different steps that we need with data science, such as collecting the data, sorting it and cleaning it off, and processing the various data points that we are working with as well. We are even able to take it a bit further and look at some of the visualizations that are needed to help showcase the data in a manner that is easier to work with.

The Pandas library is going to be a package that will come with Python and has been designed so that it can specifically make some of the work that we need with labeled and relational data simple and more intuitive. Pandas are going to be the best tool that we can use to help out with many of the processes that we want to handle, and this can include some of the data wranglings that needs to happen in this process.

In addition to some of the benefits that we have talked about before, the Pandas library is going to work well when it comes to easy and quick data visualization, manipulation, and aggregation, along with some of the other tasks that we need to work within order to help us get our work done in data science.

Matplotlib

As we are working through some of the libraries and projects that we want to focus on with data science, we are going to find that working with some data visuals can be helpful as well. These visuals are going to make it easier for us to handle the complex relationships that are found in our information and our data in the first place.

For most people, it is a lot easier to go through and understand the information that we have when it comes to some sort of visual, whether this is in a picture, in a graph or chart, or some other method. At least compared to some of the methods that we can use with reports and spreadsheets. This is why the visualization process of data is so important when it is time to work with data science. And this is why we need to look at Matplotlib to help us to take care of these visuals.

Matplotlib is going to be one of the best data science and Python libraries to work with to make sure that we can create and handle some of the simple and most powerful visuals in no time. it is going to be a really strong piece of software that will help us to take the results that we are getting when we do the algorithms, and then effortlessly turning them into something that we are able to see and understand easier than before.

We have to remember here that when we are working with the matplotlib, you will find that it is going to be low-level. This means that you are going to need to spend more time writing out more code to help all of this get done and to give us some of the higher-levels of visuals that we would like. It requires a bit more effort than we are maybe used to working with, but it is going to still provide us with some of the things that we need to get our work done. Just be aware that it does require some more work.

When we are working with this kind of library, we have to look at it to help us see how we are able to handle pretty much any kind of visual that we would like. But we have to remember that we are working with a lot of data and go through the algorithms to understand that information first. Some of the different options that you are able to work with when it comes to these visuals though will include the following:

1. The step plot
2. Contour plots
3. Quiver plots
4. Spectrograms
5. Pie charts
6. Histograms
7. Bar charts
8. Scatter plots
9. Line plots

In addition to helping you to work through some of the different plots and graphs that we have above, it is possible to work with a few of the other capabilities that happen with this language and this library. You can use this kind of library, and some of the features that we need, in order to work with creating grids, legends, and labels to make the formatting of our visuals easier to handle. There is a lot that we are going to enjoy when it is time to handle these visuals with matplotlib, and it is definitely an option that you will want to spend some of your time on.

Scikit-Learn

This is going to be an additional package that you are able to get along with the SciPy Stack that we talked about earlier on. This one was designed to help us out with a few specific functions, like image processing and facilitation of machine learning. When it comes to the latter of the two, one of the most prominent is going to be this library compared to all of the others. It is also one that is built on SciPy and will make a lot of use on a regular basis of the math operations that come with SciPy as well.

This package is a good one to work with because it can expose a concise and consistent interface that programmers are able to use when it is time to work with the ones that go with the most common algorithms of machine learning. This is going to make it simple to bring machine learning into the production system. The library is able to combine together quality code and good documentation, which can bring together high performance and ease of use, and it is one of the industry standards when it comes to doing anything that you need with machine learning in Python.

Theano

We can also spend some time working with the Theano library, and we will find how this one is going to work the best when we want to handle more of the deep learning process rather than machine learning like the other options. This library is going to be a kind of package from Python that is able to handle arrays that are more multi-dimensional, similar to what we saw with NumPy library and some of the mathematical expressions and operations.

When we work with the Theano library and we get it all compiled, which means that we get it to run as efficiently as possible on all of the architectures along the way, it is going to help us to get so much done in no time at all. This library is going to be so great with some of the deep learning that we want to accomplish, and it is worth our time if we want to focus more on the deep learning that we need.

One of the most important things that we will be able to focus on when it comes to working with the Theano library is that it is really great at integrating tightly with the NumPy library on some of the operations that are considered lower in level. The library is going to help us to optimize any of the GPU and CPU that you are working with, which is going to help us to go through these computations faster than before. Add in that this library is going to be more efficient and table and you will get precision in your results that weren't possible in the past, and you will see why this is a great option to go with.

TensorFlow

The next library on the list that we are able to talk about is going to be known as the TensorFlow library. This is going to be a library that is special because it was originally developed by Google and it is also going to be open-sourced so that we are able to use it for our own needs in no time. It also comes with computations for data flow graphs and more that have been sharpened in order to make sure that we can handle machine learning.

In addition, we are going to find that this library is going to be one of the best to choose when it is time to work with neural networks. These networks are a great type of algorithm to handle because they will help us to handle our data and make some good decisions through the system. However, we have to remember that this is not something that is only specific to Google's company. It is going to have enough power behind it and will be general-purpose enough to help us out with some applications that are better for the real-world.

One of the biggest features that we are going to need to focus on when it comes to this kind of library is that we are likely to see a lot of nodes that are in many layers when we work with the system. This is going to be great to work with because it will help us to train any of the artificial neural networks that we have, even when we have a set of data that is really large. This is going to make it easier to handle some of the models and algorithms that we are looking to create. For example, this is a library that has been used to help with voice recognition and even the identification of objects in a picture that is presented. And these are just a few of the options that we will be able to see with this kind of library.

Keras

And the final library that we are going to take a look at in this guidebook is the Keras library. This is going to be a great open-sourced library that is going to help again with some of the neural networks that we want to handle in this language, especially the ones that happen at a higher level, and it is also written in Python to make things easier. We will find that when it comes to the Keras library, the whole thing is pretty easy to work with and minimalistic, with some high-level extensibility to help us out. it is going to use the TensorFlow or Theano libraries as the back end, but right now Microsoft is working to integrate it with CNTK as a new back end to give us some more options.

Many users are going to enjoy some of the minimalistic design that comes with Keras. In fact, this kind of design is aimed at making our experimentation as easy and fast as well, because the systems that you will use will still stay compact. In addition, we will find that Keras is going to be an easy language to get started with, and it can make some of the prototyping that we want to handle easier.

We will also find that the Keras library is going to be written out in pure Python, and it is going to be a higher level just by nature, helping us to get more programming and machine learning done on our own. It is also highly extendable and modular. Despite the ease of using this library, the simplicity that comes with it, and the high-level orientation, Keras is still going to have enough power to help us get a lot of serious modeling.

The general idea that is going to come with Keras is based on lots of layers, and then everything else that you need for that model is going to be built around all of the layers. The data is going to be prepared in tensors. The first layer that comes with this is then responsible for the input of those tensors. Then the last layer however many layers this may be down the road, is going to be responsible for the output. We will find that all of the other parts of the model are going to be built in between on this to help us get the results that we would like.

As we are able to see through this chapter is that there are a ton of libraries that we are able to work in order to help us out with Python and will help us get things done when handling machine learning and all of the other parts that we want with data science. Creating some of the models that come with machine learning, and making sure that the data we have collected in the raw form is actually able to be changed around to make sense and help us to make good business decisions is so much more successful when we are able to work with some of these Python libraries to get it done.

All of the different libraries that we have spent some of our time discussing and learning about in this guidebook will be able to help us handle a lot of the different parts of the process, and will help us out in a lot of manners as well along the way. it is important as someone or some company who wants to work with data science to make sure that we are going with the best library for what kind of project that we want to handle. And you will find that all of them can help us get things done and will provide us with a lot of the tools that we are looking for as well.

Chapter 4: Gathering Your Data

The first thing that we need to take a look at is how to gather up the data that we need to accomplish this kind of process in data science. We need to have a chance to go through and look at our data, figure out what kind of data is out there that we can use, and so much more. But figuring out where to get that data, how much to collect, and what kind is going to be right to help us figure out more about our customers and industry, can be hard.

There is an overabundance of options out there when it comes to the kind of data that we want to use along the way. We need to make sure that we are picking out the right kinds of data, rather than just collecting data because it is there and looks like the right thing to work with. When we are able to organize this in the manner that we need, and we make sure that we actually get the good data, even if it is not organized and structured the way that we want in the beginning, it is going to be so important.

That is why we are going to spend some time in this chapter exploring what we are able to do with our data, how it is going to work for our needs and even some of the places where you are able to look in order to find the data that you would like to work with. With that in mind, we need to dive right in!

Know Your Biggest Business Problem

There is a lot of data out there, and it is not going to take long doing some searching before you find that you will end up in a rabbit hole with all of this information if you don't have a plan or a direction for what you are going to do with all of that information. There is a ton of good data, but if you just let it lead you rather than having a clear path in front of you, you are going to end up with a lot of problems and will never get the decision making help that you need.

If you have already gathered up your data, then this point is gone and we just need to work from there. you can form through your biggest business problem, the one that you would like to spend your time focusing on and fixing, and then sort through the data there and see what changes you are able to make and what data out of that large source you have is going to make the biggest difference. Don't be scared to just leave some of the data for later, and don't let the fact that you may not use some of the data hold you back either.

During this time, we want to focus on knowing the best information, this is going to be the best way to make sure that you get the information needed to really propel your business into the future. Even some of the information is left behind, that is fine. You may come back to it later if you need some of it. But only the best data that you have should be used for your algorithms to give you the best results.

Now, if you have not had the time to go and collect any data yet, this is something we can work with as well. Forming the problem that you would like to solve, and having a clear path can help you to sort through all of the noise that is out there, and will ensure that you are really able to get things done in the process. You need to make sure that you are searching in the right places, and looking for the information that is going to be the most critical for what you are trying to accomplish, the part that is going to be so important when it is time to handle some of the work that is out there.

Places to Look for the Data

The next thing that we need to consider when it comes to this process of gathering up the data and using it in the manner that we would like is figuring out where to find and look for the data that we need. There are actually so many different places where we are able to look for the data that we want to handle, but this is part of the beauty of the modern system that we are using today.

We have to remember though that most of the data that we will collect today is not going to be organized or structured. We will look at some of the steps that you are able to take in order to organize the data a little bit later, so this is not a big deal. Just be prepared that you will have to go through and take on a few extra steps in order to make sure that your data stays organized in the manner that you would like and that it is not going to be as nice and neat as you would like in the long run.

So, the places where you are able to look for some of the data that you would like to use in this process will be varied and it often depends on what you are hoping to get out of this process. You want to concentrate on getting the highest-quality data in the process that you can though. This is going to ensure that you are going to be able to find the data that you need and that the algorithms you use later on will really be able to provide you with some of the best results and insights that you need to move your business forward.

There are still a lot of places where you are able to look to find the data that you want. You will find that you can pick out data from websites (especially if you would like to work with web scraping), from social media sites if you are using one from surveys and focus groups of your own, and from other companies who may have collected the information and are using it to help out others along the way.

You may find that if you are able to bring up data from a more unique source as well, this is going to get you even further ahead with some of the work that you want to do. It will ensure that you will have data that no one else is going to have, and will provide you with some new patterns and insights, as long as you make sure that the data is high quality and will actually be good for your needs.

Where to Store the Data?

We also need to consider where we would like to store some of the data that we are working with along the way. You are likely to gather up a lot of data in the process, and it isn't likely that you just want to have it sitting around without a purpose or having it in a safe and secure location. This is especially true if you are working with data that is your own, data you got from surveys and other places that you don't want others getting ahold of.

There are a number of different places where you are able to store this data for your own needs and the location that you choose is often going to depend on what works for you. If you have enough storage space on your own network, this can be a great place to start. Then the data is always safe and secure with you and easy to reach. You just need to make sure that you are keeping some good security measures on your system so you don't end up losing that information and no longer having it at your disposal.

Many companies decide to put it on a web-based storage area, like the cloud. This adds in another level of protection to the information and will ensure that you are able to reach that data when you need it as well. There are a lot of these kinds of storage areas that we are able to work with, and you will find that you are able to get this to work for some of your needs pretty well. Whether your storage needs are large or not, you will find that storing this data is going to make a world of difference when it is time to handle this process, and you just have to decide how much you would like to use ahead of time.

Knowing where to find the data that you need to start out with your data analysis and data science project is going to be super important. This is going to set the tone for the work that you are able to do later on and how much success you are going to have with your project as well. Make sure to search around for the data that is going to be needed in this, and pay attention to how much of it you will need, where you are likely to find it, and more.

Chapter 5: Organizing and Cleaning the Data

As you get into the process of working with data science, you will quickly find that the vast majority of your time with a project is going to be spent collecting, cleaning, and then preparing the data that you have to work in analysis. This is because many times, the sets of data that we have are going in a lot of sizes, formats, and more, and if they are not organized and ready to go, you are going to run into some problems with getting the project to work, and ensuring that you get accurate results.

This is why we will want to spend some time cleaning and organizing the data that we are working with along the way. there are a number of methods that you are able to use to make this work for your needs. But in the end we want to make sure that we have the data organized, usually in a database of some kind, the duplicates handled and gotten rid of, and we need to have a plan for some of the missing values and outliers that are found in your data. Let's dive into some of the basics of data preparation and why this is so important to some of the work that you need to do in a data science project.

What is Data Preparation?

Let's say that we are going through and trying to get a good analysis of the log files that are on a website so that we can figure out which IP address a spammer is coming from. You can also use this to figure out which demographics your website is reaching and getting more sales with, or which region geographically your website is the most popular in. What steps would we need to take in order to figure these things out?

To help us to answer all of these kinds of questions, we need to perform an analysis of the data and we need to do this with a few important columns. This is going to include the number of hits that a website gets, and the IP address of the hit. As we know, the log files that we may use are not going to be structured and this means that we will have to go through and sort out the unstructured information as best we can. This requires some work and some good organization and cleaning in order to make it all work out.

The idea of data preparation is where we are able to take all of that data that is kind of a mess and doesn't have the formatting and more that we want, and we turn it into a form that is easy to use and will flow through our chosen algorithms later on if we would like. This does require a number of steps in order to be successful, and often it is not fun.

For example, there are a lot of studies out there to look at this part of the data science project, and it is going to be really hard to miss out on this step. In fact, it is estimated that when it comes to a data science project, you will spend up to 60 percent of your time organizing and cleaning the data. This is compared to all of the other steps having to take up other parts of the process, and it is pretty amazing how important this process is.

The reason that this process is so important is that it needs to have clean and organized data in order to get things done. If the data is a mess, and if there are a lot of outliers or information that does not match up the way that it should, it is going to be a waste of time. The algorithm will not be able to go through the process in the right manner, and it is going to provide you with answers that are not accurate.

For example, if you go through and find that there are a lot of missing or duplicate values, then this can really skew the information that you are getting out of this information. If there are a lot of duplicates, then the information and the results will start to skew a bit towards this one as well. On the other hand, if you end up with a good average, but then you see that there are a few outliers that really are far away from this average, it could mess with some of the results as well.

This is why cleaning up the data is going to be so important. We want to make sure that the results we are putting into the algorithms, and the outputs that it gives out t us in the end, are going to be accurate. Many companies are going to base a lot of business decisions on these results, so the more time that we can spend cleaning that data and keeping it as organized and easy to use as possible is going to ensure that the algorithms work the way that we want.

However, you will find that even though the cleaning and preparation process is going to be so important, it is not much fun. About 57 percent of data scientists out there find that cleaning and organizing the data, even when it is so important, is going to be one of the most boring and least enjoyable tasks that come with this process.

Why Is Data Preparation So Important?

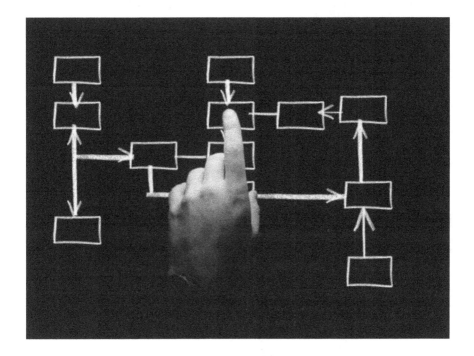

To see why this is so important, we need to take a look at an example of how this can work. Let's say that you are working as a data scientist and you are going to need to estimate how many burgers your store is going to sell on a daily basis. You are going to work with a file that will have rows that will describe some of the financial information about the system.

There are going to also be some columns like state, city, and how many of the burgers are sold.

However, rather than having all of this data show up in one document, it is likely that information is going to be split up in a lot of different files, and most of them are going to come in a lot of different formats so it is difficult to look it all over or combine them with one another.

This is the job of a data scientist. They will need to join together all of the data and make sure that the combinations they get make sense so they can continue on with the analysis. Usually, there are going to be several formatting inconsistencies and floating issues that show up in the set of data. For example, there are going to be some rows where you see that the state is going to be 101 and then the number of burgers could be something like New York. This is a mess, but it is sometimes what happens when we move things around and try to combine them with one another. And that is exactly why we need to work with the process of data cleaning.

Data cleaning is a process that is going to require that the data scientist goes through and finds all of the glitches, fixes them up, and then make sure that the next time this information comes in, it is going to automatically be fixed along the way. predictive analysis results of a data scientist can be as good as the data they have assembled. Data preparation is going to be vital and important to the process that you are doing and can help us to actually find some of the insights that we are looking for out of that data.

With all of the great data that we are able to gather over time, you will find that the problem isn't finding the data that you need. The problem is going to be making sure that the data is organized and ready to work with when you would like. This takes some time, but high-quality data is going to be the backbone of some of the things that you want to do with this process. Making sure that the data is high quality and will work the way that you want is going to be important to this as well.

Steps Involved for Data Preparation

There are a few steps that we are able to work with when it is time to handle this process of data preparation. The first one is going to be where we work on data cleaning. This is where we are going to spend our time correcting some of the data that is not consistent and then filling out some of the missing values while smoothing out some of the data that is making a lot of noise.

Keep in mind with this one that there could be a lot of rows in the set of data that are not going to have value for attributes of interest, or there could be some data that is not consistent or has duplicate records. And sometimes it is just another random error to work with as well. All of these data quality issues are going to be tackled when we are in this kind of process.

The missing values are going to be tackled in a lot of different manners depending on the requirements that we find. This can happen when we either ignore the tuple or when we work to fill in the value that is missing with the mean value of the attribute. There are a few other options that we are able to use for this one such as the global constant, the Bayesian formula, or the decision tree. Noisy data is something that we are able to tackle manually through a lot of regression or clustering techniques.

The second step that we need to focus on here is going to be known as data integration. This one is going to involve a number of steps to help us get some of the work done that we need including schema integration, resolving data conflicts if there are any there, and then handling redundancies in the data.

The third step that comes up when we are preparing our data is data transformation. This is a step that requires us taking away any of the noise that is found in our data. When that noise is done, we can then work on normalization, aggregation, and then generalization of the data to help us get the results that you would like.

The next thing that we are able to work with is going to be known as data reduction. The data warehouse is going to contain some petabytes of the data and then running the analysis on the complete data that is present in the warehouse. This is going to be a process that is really time-consuming. In this step, the data scientist is going to obtain a reduced representation of the set of data, that is going to be smaller in size, but yields are going to be almost the same as the outcomes of the analysis.

When we are working on this step, you will find that there are a number of data reduction methods that you are able to apply to your data. The kind that you are going to use will often depend on the requirements that you have with some of the results that you are able to work with this. Some of the data reduction methods that you are able to work with will include numerosity reduction, data cube aggregation, and dimensionality reduction.

And finally, the final step that we are able to work with when it is time to do some of our data cleanings is going to be the data discretization. The set of data that you are going to work with will often contain three-man types of attributes. These attributes are going to include ordinal, nominal, and continuous to talk about a few.

It is possible that some algorithms are going to only go through and accept attributes that are categorical. Data discretization is going to be a step that is good for helping the data scientist to divide up some of their continuous attributes so that they fall in smaller intervals and will make it smaller in size as well. This is one of the best ways to make sure that the data is going to be set up and ready for you to use.

As you can see here, there are going to be a lot of techniques and methods that you are able to use and many more that are developed to help out with the preparation of your data in this stage. But it is still very much in the early stages of what we can do, and many data scientists are still working with it in order to find some new strategies and techniques that they are able to use for some of their own needs.

It is so important for you to spend time learning how to clean off the data that you are working with overall. This is going to make a world of difference in how successful you are going to be with some of your work, and will ensure that the data is going to actually be ready for some of the algorithms that you are going to work with later on.

The data cleaning process is going to take up quite a bit of the time that you need for your data science and data analysis process, even though it may not be as fun to work with as some of the other parts along the way. making sure that you are set up and ready to handle some of the work that comes with it, and understanding why this process is so important in the first place, is going to be so important to ensure that you get the results that you would like along the way. follow some of the steps that are in this chapter, and you will be able to clean and organize the data in the way that you need, ensuring that all of that data is ready to go when it is time to handle your data analysis.

Chapter 6: A Look at Data Mining

Another topic that we need to spend some time on here is a bit of the work that comes with data mining. This is going to be a new topic that we haven't had a lot of time to talk about yet. But it is going to be a specific part of the data science process that we need to focus on, and we need to take a closer look in order to help us get the data working and performing the way that we want. That is why we are going to take a look at why this data mining is so important and what we are able to do with it.

The first goal that we want to focus on when we are working with this idea of data mining is to learn more about what this process is. data mining is going to be the steps that a company is going to use in order to take all of the raw data that they have, and turn it around into information that is useful. It is going to be a bit more specialized than the original steps we talked about in the first chapter. But with some of the work that we can do with machine learning, Python, and a good type of software, a company is going to work with data mining to help look for some patterns that will show up in the larger batches of data.

The reason that we want to take some time to look through all of this data and see what is inside of it is that there is often quite a bit of data that we need to go through to start with. Businesses are able to look through a lot of data, and hopefully, if the data mining works well and does what they would like, they will be able to learn something new. Whether they learn how to better serve their customers, how to beat out the competition, and even how to develop some marketing strategies that are better, it is going to help us to increase sales, cut down on costs, and really help to reduce the risks as much as possible.

There are a lot of parts that we have to make sure comes together if we would like to make sure that the process of data mining is going to work the way that we would like. There are a number of steps that we are able to take a look at when it is time to work on the process of data mining, and this is going to include a few things including collecting enough data, warehousing, and processing power on the system of your computer.

The Process of Data Mining

Using some of the information that we have above, and keeping that in mind, we need to spend some time looking at the basics of what we have with data mining overall. Data mining is going to involve a company going through the process of exploration and then analyzing a large amount of the information, in the hopes of figuring out some of the patterns and trends in the data that are the most important and meaningful. As we can imagine, it is likely that they are going to be able to find a ton of insights and some other information that is valuable inside of all that.

There are a lot of methods that companies are going to be able to help them get through all of this information, including managing the risk of credit if someone wants to borrow money, doing marketing through the database, detecting fraud, and filtering out emails that are spam. It could even be used to help figure out the sentiments and opinions of those who are on your system. All of these, when pulled out and accurate, can help you to gain a good advantage over the competition with your company.

Of course, we have to start somewhere, and this place is with the enormous process of data mining. This data mining is going to help us to break down all of the information in some easy steps that we can follow. To get this to work for our needs, we are going to make it simple and work with five steps that are easy to learn and work with and can help make sure that we get the most out of it.

The first step of this process is that the company is going to go through and collect the data that they need, and then load it up into the warehouse, or another storage area, that they want to use to keep ahold of that information. The type of data that you want to collect is going to be based on what information you would like, and what your overall goal is when you get started with this process as well.

The second step is that we would like to make sure that we are storing and managing the data in the right manner. This is usually going to be done either through the cloud or with some servers that the company is using on their own. Management teams, business analysts, and information technology professionals are then able to access the data and determine the best method that they can use in order to organize all of that data and learn more information from it.

Then, the company needs to go through and figure out what kind of application software they want to use. There are a number of these that are available for the programmer to choose from, and they can often work with machine learning and the Python coding language to help get the work done. The application software is going to help us to sort out all of the data that we are working on, based on the results form the user.

When all of this is done, the end-user is going to be able to take all of the insights and the information that they have been able to gather up, and then present that data and all of their findings to those who need it. Usually, this needs to be done in a format that is really easy to share, including a table or a graph, so that it is easier for those key people, the ones who really need to use the information, to see what insights are there.

Data mining is going to be a discipline that is able to help us represent a variety of techniques and methods that are used in capabilities that are more analytic than others. This is going to be a useful process because it is able to help us to address a ton of the needs that come in the company, and you can spend some of that time asking different questions and use different levels of human rules or inputs in order to come up with this decision. There are going to be some parts that will come into play when we work with the process of data mining, and a few of these will include:

Descriptive modeling: This is going to be one of the first parts of data mining that we are able to use in our process. When we work with this kind of modeling, we will find that it is responsible for uncovering some of the groupings or similarities that are shared in all of our historical data. This will help us determine the reasons that are behind the failure or the success of a company.

For example, we are able to use this to make it easier to categorize the customers that we are working with. Maybe we will do this by the preference that these customers have to the products that our company is selling or to some of their sentiments overall. There are a variety of techniques that we are able to use to make this happen and that will fit into the idea of descriptive modeling, and some of the ones that we are able to focus on here will include:

1. Clustering: This is when we are able to group some of the records that are similar to one another.
2. Anomaly detection: This is when we are going to work to identify some of the outliers, and then will determine whether these are important and should be looked at a bit more closely or not.

3. Association rule learning: This is when we are going to take some of the records that we have and detect whether there are some kinds of relationships between them and what those relationships are.

4. Principal component analysis: This is where we are going to take a look to detect what kind of relationship is going to be present with the variables that we are working on.

5. Affinity grouping: This is when we group people together who have a common interest or simple goals at the same time.

Of course, we are able to look at this from another angle as well if we would like. The second part of all this that we are able to focus our attention on is the idea of predictive modeling. This is going to be modeling that is useful because it will go deeper in order to classify some of the events that may happen in the future. It is also a good way to help us estimate some of the outcomes that are not known ahead of time.

A good example of this one would be how we are able to work with credit scoring to make it easier to determine how likely someone is to repay their loan, or if they are more likely to default on that loan ahead of time. The idea that comes with these predictive modeling is that it is going to ensure that we are able to uncover all of the patterns and the various insights that we need in order to make decisions that are better for us. Some of the insights that we are likely to see here will include the response of a campaign we sent out for marketing, the likelihood of credit default, and even customer churn.

There are going to be a few different techniques that we are able to focus on when it comes to using this option for our needs. Some of the options here for techniques that fit under the term of predictive modeling are going to include:

1. Regression: This is going to be a measure of the strength that we see between one dependent variable and a series of variables that are independent.

2. Neural networks: This is a complicated type of computer program that can be set up in order to learn, make its own predictions, and even detect some of the patterns that are found in your own data as well.

3. Decision trees; These are going to be a type of diagram, that is shaped like a tree, that can help you to make some decisions. The point with this one is that you are able to take a look at each of the branches and see the probable occurrence of each part. This helps us to see which one is the best option for us when making a decision.

4. Support vector machine: This is going to be an example of a supervised learning model from machine learning that can help our model to learn the way that it should.

And finally, there is another process that we need to look at a bit more here that is known as prescriptive modeling. Thanks to all of the growth that is going on in our world when it comes to unstructured data and more, and all of the things that we are able to do with this kind of data, the prescriptive modeling option is going to grow a lot in popularity.

Think right now about all of the different sources of data that is unstructured out there that we are able to work with. And these come to us in formats including books, comment fields, web emails, PDFs, audio, and more. This is useful information to work with, but it is going to need some data mining so that we are able to sort through it and really see what information is inside to help us out.

It is important for us to have a successful method that will help us to parse, filter, and then transform all of this data so that we can really see what is inside of it and add it to our predictive models. It may seem like a lot of extra work along the way, but it is so important to these models because it is going to improve the amount of accuracy that we are going to see with some of the predictions that we make.

In the end, it is so important that we learn how to take a look at data mining, not just as its own separate entity when it comes to data science. It is just as important as some of the others, and it is not a step that we need to miss out on when we are accomplishing some of our work along the way. But it is something that we need to focus our attention on and ensure that we are not going to miss out on if we really want to learn what is going on in our data and how we are able to use the data.

A Look at Data Warehousing

Another topic that we need to spend a bit more time on while we are here is the idea of data warehousing and some of the mining software that we are able to use. You will quickly find that programs for data mining are going to be used quite a bit by a lot of companies, and they are going to be there in order to make it easier for us to analyze the patterns and the relationships that are found in all of the unstructured data that we have. usually, this is going to be done based on the requests that come in from the user. For example, a company is going to be able to use this kind of software to make it easier for them to create classes of information that would help them get things done.

To help us to illustrate this point, let's imagine that there is a restaurant that we want to follow, one who is interested in using some of the processes that come with data mining in order to make it easier to offer the right specials at the right time. They want to make sure that these specials will hit the right customers and make them the most money possible in the process. This company is going to take a look at all of the information that it has been able to collect and then will create some classes, based on when a customer came to eat, and what they ended up ordering.

Of course, this is just one example of how we are able to use the process of data mining to improve our business. In some other situations, a data miner is able to find a cluster of information based on a logical relationship, or they will look at the associations and sequential patterns in order to draw up a few conclusions about trends that are seen in consumer behavior.

While we are doing this though, we have to remember some of the reasons why we need to focus on warehousing when we do some of our own data mining. Warehousing may sound strange, but it is going to be a simple process where a company is able to pick out one database or type of software in order to centralize all of the raw data that they are focusing on.

With the help of this kind of warehouse to hold the data, the company is able to spin off some of the segments of data that they need over to the right users. These users can then have the right kind of data and use it in analysis, preparing it and getting things ready when it is needed.

However, it is also possible in some situations that we end up in that the analysis is going to start out with some of the data already in place, the data that they want to work with, and then it is possible to work on creating one of these warehouses based on those specifications already from the start. Regardless of how business and some of the other entities out there are going to choose to store and organize their own data, they still want to make sure that they are using it in a manner that is going to support the management decisions later on.

As we can see already, there is a ton of stuff that we are able to do when it comes to working with the data mining process. It may sound like a strange process to work within the beginning and like it is not worth our time, but being able to go through and understand the data that we have and what it all means is going to be so important along the way.

This is going to be the part that shows up in our project of data science that we really need to spend some time focusing on. This is because it will help us to get a better understanding of some of the data that we have and what we can do wit it. When we are done with this particular process, we will find that we will have the best possible understanding of that information and how we are able to run it through the algorithm of our choice to get the most out of it all.

Chapter 7: Adding Machine Learning to the Mix

While we are on this topic, we need to spend a bit of time taking a look at something known as machine learning. This is going to be a really important part of the whole process because it allows us to take all of the information that we have, the information that we have spent a lot of time collecting, organizing, and learning more about, and then puts it through some of the algorithms that will tell us more about the information overall. While all of the steps in this process are going to be really important to help us to gain the insights and patterns that we need for some smart decision making, you will find that this is sometimes considered the fun part, the part that is going to help us to actually put that data to good use.

And we are able to accomplish this with the help of machine learning. This chapter is going to spend some time looking at this buzz word that has taken over the world of business in so many ways. Despite this though, there are a lot of people who have to know the idea of what machine learning is all about or even how they can use machine learning in order to reach some of their own business goals in no time.

To help us get started here, you will find that looking closely at machine learning and what it is all about, and why it is so popular in the world of business today is an important step to get started with. For this one, machine learning is going to be one of the applications of artificial intelligence that will provide our systems with the ability to automatically learn and improve from experience, without us programming it on everything that we want it to be doing in the process. Machine learning is going to focus on the development of computer programs that are going to access data, and then will be able to use this data to help it to learn.

The process of learning in machine learning is going, to begin with, observations, or even data, such as instructions, direct experiences, and examples, in order to look for patterns in data and make better decisions in the future based on the example that we provide. The primary aim is to allow these computers a way to automatically learn without any assistance or intervention from humans, and then you can see that the computer will be able to adjust their actions accordingly to work with this as well.

There are a lot of applications that go with machine learning, and we are going to spend some of our time in this guidebook looking at a lot of the different algorithms and more that you are able to do with machine learning. When you are able to get all of this working together, you will see some amazing results and really see the true potential that comes with machine learning.

There are a lot of different things that you are able to use in machine learning. Any time that you aren't sure how the end result is going to turn up, or you aren't sure what the input of the other person could be, you will find that machine learning can help you get through some of these problems. If you want the computer to be able to go through a long list of options and find patterns or find the right result, then machine learning is going to work the best for you. Some of the other things that machine learning can help out with include:

1. Voice recognition
2. Facial recognition
3. Search engines. The machine learning program is going to start learning from the answers that the individual provides, or the queries, and will start to give better answers near the top as time goes on.

4. Recommendations after shopping
5. Going through large amounts of data about finances and customers and making accurate predictions about what the company should do to increase profits and happy customers along the way.

Of course, these are just going to be a handful of the times when we would want to rely on machine learning and what it is able to do for us. We can easily see that some of the traditional programs that we are learning how to use as a beginner are going to be too simplistic in order to handle this. They have to work by telling the computer exactly what it should do in a specific situation. And this does work great for a lot of the programs that you want to write. But when you want to add in some artificial intelligence to the mix, you will find that this really is not going to be enough for what you want to do.

In addition, you may find that machine learning is a good thing to use when it is time to handle any of your data analysis, and other parts of a data science project. This part is going to come into play when we need to handle some of the basic and more complex algorithms that are out there in machine learning. There are a lot of algorithms that are going to happen with this one, but knowing how to work with these, and how they fit in with data science and machine learning is going to be important.

Why Should I Use Machine Learning?

As you start to gain some more familiarity with the world of machine learning, you will quickly see that there are a number of benefits of working with the various parts of machine learning. This is probably one of the main reasons that so many companies are interested in machine learning and making it work for their needs. Depending on the questions that you would like to see answered for your company and more, you will find that machine learning can be applied to your business in no time.

To help us out with this, machine learning is going to really help us to simplify some of the steps that come with marketing a product and can even help when it is time to make forecasts on future sales that are more accurate. Machine learning is able to help us out in many ways when it is time to do some of these tasks and more. For example, you will find that going through all of the data that you have collected manually is going to be hard. There is a ton of information in that data for you to explore and learn from, but doing it in a manual way is going to take a lot of time and be really hard to accomplish.

This is where machine learning is going to come into play as well. It is going to give us a look at what insights and patterns are actually in the data, along with some of the past trends that we need to worry about as well. And it is able to do all of this at a much faster rate than we are used to seeing in some of the other parts of our process or by doing it by hand as well.

All of these things are going to come together and ensure that we get some of the results that we would like in no time. you can use this unlimited amount of information to help learn a bit more about your customers and what they would like out of your business, learn the best way to reach them in some of the marketing that you do, what the competition is doing that is so successful and more. Since marketing and all of these other parts are going to be so important in some of the work that you need to do to grow your business, we can already see why machine learning may be the option that you want to go with to get the best results.

In addition, we will find that machine learning is also going to be there to help facilitate some of the predictions and diagnoses that are done in the medical field. This kind of machine learning is a good way for doctors to identify the patients who are at the highest risk for some kinds of diseases, can help us get the best medicine for each case, and so much more.

The way that these programs will work is that they are based on some of the available sets of data on patients, all that is kept anonymous at the time as well, and then it is compared to some of the symptoms that the patient is going through at the time. this is going to help doctors, as well as other medical professionals you work with, add in more precision and efficiency to the job that they are doing. And this is just one of the areas where machine learning is able to help out in the medical field.

Data entry, especially when it is done on a really large set of data, is going to be important but it is going to take too long to accomplish in a manual manner. This is going to be something else that machine learning will be able to step in and help out with. Data duplication and inaccuracy is a big issue that comes up when we do all of this data entry by hand, but automating the process with machine learning can get it done in a quick and efficient manner, and will ensure that it is as accurate as possible.

Another area that we are going to see this machine learning technology do really well is in the financial world. Some of the most common benefits that we will see when we do some research on machine learning in the financial world are going to include fraud detection, algorithmic trading, underwriting of loans and so much more in the process.

In addition, this is the kind of learning that is going to help us with something known as continual data assessments. This is used to help us detect and then analyze some of the anomalies that are going to show up in the financial world, and will help us to improve the precision that we are able to find in our models and other parts as well.

We will also see that machine learning is able to help with detecting spam. This was actually one of the earliest problems that machine learning was able to come in and help with. Spam filters are able to make up new rules, using neural networks, in order to eliminate spam mail and keep your inbox as clean as possible. The neural network is able to learn how to recognize phishing messages as well as other junk mail when it evaluates the rules that are found across an ever-growing network of computers.

The manufacturing industry is even able to benefit from some of the things that we see with machine learning. Manufacturing firms need to have corrective and preventative maintenance practices in place. However, these are going to be inefficient and costly in many cases. This is where machine learning can step in to help, and it is going to be a great tool in creating a highly efficient predictive maintenance plan that keeps the business up and running and doing well. In fact, when the company follows these plans, it is going to minimize the chances of failures that are not expected to happen, which will reduce unnecessary preventive maintenance activities.

Machine learning is also going to help with better customer segmentation and accurate lifetime value prediction. These are going to be some of the biggest challenges that marketers are going to face on a daily basis today. Marketing and sales units are going to have an enormous amount of data sourced from many channels, but accurate predictions are only going to be found when we look at machine learning.

These are just a few of the benefits that we will be able to work with when it is time to bring out some of the machine learning that we would like to do. And there is so much more that is going to come into play when we use this into the future and figure out the specific ways that we are able to make data science and machine learning go together.

Now that we know a few of the benefits that are available, it is time for us to dive a bit more into machine learning. In specific, we are going to take a look at the three main types of machine learning, and how each of them is meant to work for some of our needs within this kind of field as well. For the most part, we are going to focus on supervised machine learning, which is going to be all about training the models that we have with examples. Then there is also unsupervised machine learning, where we train the algorithm to work by finding the patterns and more that are there all on its own. And finally, we have the reinforcement machine learning that is able to do all of the necessary learning through trial and error.

Supervised Machine Learning

Now that we have had a chance to take a look at machine learning and all that it is going to entail, it is now time for us to really dive into some of this a bit more, and see what we are able to do to make it work for our needs. The first type of machine learning that we are going to spend our time on is known as supervised machine learning. These kinds of algorithms are going to apply some of the information that we have been able to learn about in the past and then will put that knowledge towards some of the new data that we have. This is often done with the help of labeled examples, to help us out with predicting whether something is likely to happen in the future or not.

Starting off with an analysis that happens on a set of data that we know about and uses for training, the algorithm of supervised machine learning that you use here is going to be able to give us a good function to make predictions about any of the values that we give it later on. The system, when we have set it up in the proper manner, is going to be able to provide us with some targets for the new input after you are done with the right amount of training.

From there, the learning algorithm is able to compare the output that it gives with the correct output. And it is also going to be able to find out any of the errors that are there so that it can make some modifications to itself along the way, and provide some better predictions so you know that you can trust it as well.

This is also going to bring up an additional type of machine learning that we are able to work with. This one is going to talk about semi-supervised machine learning. This one is able to combine together what we are talking about with supervised machine learning above, and will add in a bit of the unsupervised machine learning that we will talk about below when we are ready.

For this one to work, it is going to take some of the labeled and unlabeled data and use this in the training that we want to accomplish. in most cases, the labeled data is going to be just a small part of what is being used, and the majority of the data is going to be unlabeled. The reason for this one is that the labeled data, while useful and more efficient, is harder to find and more expensive, and it is often easier to use a combination of the two to help get work done.

The systems that work with supervised and even semi-supervised learning are going to really have more accuracy found in them compared to some of the other options, but there are some limitations that come with it, which is why we have some of the other options to work with as well. This is the type of machine learning that you will want to choose to use when you are able to get ahold of enough labeled data so that the algorithm is easily able to learn as well. Otherwise, the unlabeled data is going to come into play and you will need to focus on semi-supervised or unsupervised machine learning in order to get the work done.

Unsupervised Machine Learning

Now that we have had a chance to take a look at what the supervised machine learning algorithms are able to do, it is time to take a look at what we are able to do with unsupervised machine learning algorithms. These are going to be the ones that we use any time that the information we have is used to train the algorithm, and it is not going to be labeled or classified. This means that the algorithm, and the system or machine it is on, will need to do the learning on their own, without examples and labeled data to help it make more sense.

Unsupervised learning studies how a system is able to infer a function to describe one of the hidden structures from the unlabeled data. The system doesn't figure out the right output with this one, but it is going to explore the data and then can draw some inferences from the sets of data to describe the hidden structures from the data that is unlabeled.

With this one, we are going to use a lot of data that doesn't have a label on it or any information as to the right answer, and then we are able to send it right through the algorithm and let the system learn along the way. this takes more time and you may end up with some more runs of training and testing before you are done, but it can be one of the best ways to get some strong systems in place to help with your machine learning.

There are a lot of really neat things that we are able to do when it comes to working with unsupervised machine learning. For example, we are able to bring out some algorithms, like the neural networks, that will help us to get things done and learn along the way, without someone having to train the algorithms or teach them all of the steps along the way at all.

Reinforcement Machine Learning

And the final type of machine learning that we are going to spend some time on here is the idea of reinforcement learning. This one is going to be a method of learning that will be able to interact with the environment that is going on around it and then will produce various actions. This helps the algorithm to discover the errors or rewards that it can get based on these actions.

A good way to compare how this one is going to work is through the idea of trial and error and how we are able to learn from that method. This kind of trial and error is going to add to the search and delayed reward and this learning will be able to make sure that it does what you would like along the way in no time.

When we decide that reinforcement machine learning is the right one for our needs, it is going to be a good one that will allow the machine, as well as the other agents of software that you are using, to act on their own automatically in order to figure out what kind of behave they should exhibit based on the context that it is in. The goal is that this can happen while maximizing the performance that is seen. It works based on some of the simple reward feedback to the agent so that the agent is able to learn what is best along the way. This is going to be known as the reinforcement signal.

When we take a closer look at this kind of machine learning, there are going to be quite a few similarities that will show up between how the computer learns compared to how a human can learn along the way. This method is set up to help us really work through the process of trial and error, and then the computer is going to be able to use this idea to help them figure out the course of action that will make it the most successful. The more times that it is able to go through this process and be successful, the better it will get with it all and the more accurate the results overall.

As we can see, there are a lot of benefits that are going to show up when we are working with machine learning and all of the things that we are able to do with this kind of learning over time. The more that we want to work with data science and some of the neat things that this process, and the algorithms that are attached to it, are able to do, the more that we will want to focus on machine learning and what this can handle.

There is so much that we can potentially do when it is time to handle some of the machine learning that we want to work with and helping us to figure out the different parts, and how all of them work independently and together, will be a challenge that many data scientists are going to deal with on a regular basis. When it is possible to explore more about machine learning, and some of the different parts that you are able to handle with this language, you will be able to get so much done and really see some of the power that is available through this kind of language as well.

Chapter 8: Completing the Data Analysis

The next step that we need to spend some time on when it comes to working in data science is the idea of the data analysis. This is going to be a fun part to work with because it allows us to learn more about our data and get into some of the different things that we need to know, such as the actual insights and patterns that are in the data.

This is the part where we will actually have a chance to learn a bit about the data. Rather than having to just guess at the data or go through and gather and clean it as we did in the other steps, we now get a chance to send it through the right algorithms and hope that it comes out right on the other side.

Of course, there are a number of steps that have to happen to allow us a chance to get accurate results overall, but you will find that working with a data analysis is going to really help us to handle some of the machine learning algorithms we want to use, and learn more about our data than ever before.

With some of this in mind, we need to take some time to explore more about data analysis and what we are able to do with it in our data science project.

What is Data Analysis?

To keep it simple, data analysis is going to be the practice where a company can take their raw data and then order and organize it. When the data is organized in this manner, and run through a predictive model, it is going to help the company extract useful information out of it. The process of organizing and thinking about our data is going to be very important as it is the key to helping us understand what the data does and does not contain at any given time.

Many companies have been collecting data for a long time. They may gather this data from their customers, from surveys, from social media, and many other locations. And while collecting the data is an important step that we need to focus on as well, another thing to consider is what we can do with the data. You can collect all of the data that you would like, but if it just sits in your cloud or a data warehouse and is never mined or used, then it is going to become worthless to you, and you wasted a lot of time and money trying to figure it all out.

This is where data analysis will come in. it is able to take all of that raw data and actually, put it to some good use. It will use various models and algorithms, usually with the help of machine learning and Python, in order to help us to understand what important insights and information are found in our data, and how we are able to utilize these for our own benefit.

You will find that there are a lot of options that we can use when picking out methods to help with data analysis. Often it is not whether the options work, but more about whether they will work on the specific data or the specific problem that we would like to handle along the way. With this in mind, we have to make sure that we carefully choose the right kind of data to go through the information, and we need to make sure that we are not manipulating the data at all.

What we mean with this one is that it is really easy to bring in some of our own thoughts and opinions about the data before we even start. Sometimes we do this on purpose and other times we may not realize that it is going on at all. But if we are not careful, we will let these manipulations get into the results, and the way that we do things, and then the end results are not going to be as accurate as we would like. Keep all of the biases and the manipulations out, and you will find that the data analysis is going to be better than ever before.

One of the other things that we should really consider when we are doing some of our work here is the quality of the raw data that we are going to use. You will find that the raw data that you choose is going to take on a lot of different forms, and the sources that you use will often depend on your own unique needs and what you are hoping to accomplish from this in the process. You may look on social media posts, focus groups, study groups surveys, websites, and more. These are all great sources, and could potentially help you to get the information that you are looking for.

Once you have been able to gather up that data in the raw form, you will find that even though it is kind of a mess and all over the place, it is still going to be useful for your business to learn and grow. In addition, it is also going to seem overwhelming. This is where the data analysis is going to come into play. It allows us to take some of the workout and some of the intense amount of data, and actually learn from it without feeling overwhelmed or giving up.

When we have all of that raw data in the right form, you will find that this is going to be information that we can use, even though it may not look like it in the beginning. For example, we may find that if we go through and send out a survey to some of our customers, we may get a mess back with lots of answers from people all over the place. But when we have someone go through and sort the answers out, we are able to better see what is going on and can use that information to help us get ahead of the game.

During that unique process of working to get the data as organized as possible, it is likely that you may notice that there are a few big trends that are emerging as well. These trends are going to be important for us to focus on because they will help us to learn more about which decisions to make, how to work on your business, how to reach your customers, and more. And all of that from some data that may have seemed a bit crazy and all over the place when we first got started.

We can take a look at an example of how this is going to work. When we look at a causal survey about ice cream and what preferences men and women have with this, you may find that more women compared to men had a fondness for eating strawberry ice cream. Depending on what you are doing this whole process for and what results you are hoping to get, it could end up being a major point of interest for the researcher.

Once we know this kind of relationship is in place, we are then able to work with the process of modeling the data. This can be done with a variety of tools, including mathematics, and if you use them in the right way, it is possible that these are going to exaggerate the points of interest so that we can see them a bit easier as we go through this process.

Once we have had some time to go through all of this information and highlight some of the big trends that are found in our data, it is time to work with how it is going to be presented. Of course, we will want to do some kind of textual writeup of the information. This ensures that the people using it to make big decisions are able to see the information and understand what is there. This text needs to include information on the process you took, the resources that you used, and more. This is an important part to add to the process because it ensures that we are going to be able to get the best results and will help whoever is looking at the information to have some background to research as well.

Another thing that we are going to explore a bit more in a later chapter here is that we should add in at least a few visuals to this as well. Options are abundant here and can include things like graphs and charts. With all of the complex information and relationships that are going to show up in some of the work that we are doing, you may find that you are able to really make some of this work for your needs when you can see it in a graphic format.

If you leave it in the reports and in other documents, it may make sense, but it will take a long time to get through all of that information in order to find out those patterns and insights that you are trying to work with. A much better option to focus on here is going to be to bring in the visuals. These visuals can tell us in just a few minutes the relationships that are found in the documents and in all of that data, something that could take the document a few hours to help explain to us.

This doesn't mean that we need to ignore the reports and do nothing with them. There are plenty of times when these reports are going to be important and we don't want to forget them at all. But we do have to remember that these reports are a good summary of the information, and nothing is able to summarize data better than some good charts or graphs or another visual that works with the data that you have. Have the reports be the backup that helps to explain what is going on with the data, and then have the graphs and charts there to help give us a good idea of the relationships at a glance.

There is so much that has to go on with the data analysis phase of this process, and it is important for us to take some time to learn how this works, and what we are able to do with it. This is basically where we are able to take all of the hard work that we have done in some of the other chapters of this guidebook and put it to use. This is the fun part that includes some of the machine learning, Python, and algorithms to help us see what information is inside.

If we did a good job with some of the other parts of this process and we got this set up in the manner that it should, with high-quality, accurate, and clean information, then we will find that the data analysis phase is going to be a lot easier to work with overall. You will then find that it is easier to pick out the algorithm that you want to work with, train it and test it, and then put the data through to help you make some of the best business decisions possible.

Steps in a Data Analysis?

Now that we have had some time to talk about what the data analysis is all about and why it is so important to some of the work that we are trying to do within our business, it is time for us to take this a bit further and look closer at some of the steps that you are able to take when we work with this data analysis in the first place. There are actually a number of steps that we will want to take in order to work through this data analysis, and making sure that we get through the right steps, and use them in the right manner, is going to be so critical to ensuring we actually get the right predictions and patterns when we are all done. Some of the steps that we need to follow when working with data analysis will include the following:

1. Figuring out what business problem we would like to solve. Whether you have already done a lot of the gathering that is needed of your chosen date, or you are just starting out and you want to know which type of data is the best to gather, you first need to go through and figure out which business problem you would like to solve. This can help to direct the way that this process goes, and ensures that you

keep on track with the kind of information that you bring in.

2. Searching for the data that we want to work with. Once we have a good idea of the information that we need, and the business problem that we would like to solve, it is time for us to go through and look for the data. There are a number of places where we are able to find this data, such as in surveys, social media, and more, so going out and searching for it here is going to be the best way to gather it up and have it ready to work with on the later steps.

3. Cleaning and organizing our data. Since we are usually gathering our data from a lot of different places, and it is often going to come to us in a more unstructured form, it is always a good idea to go through and clean and organize that data. This will make it easier for us to putt that data through the algorithm that we want to use and to make sure that it will all work out.

4. Making sure the outliers, missing values, and any duplication information is removed. All of these things are possible to find in your data, and in the beginning, they are not going to seem like they are that big of a deal. But the more of these that are there, the more they are going to mess with some of the results that you are able to get out of your

algorithms. We need to spend some time searching through the data to see if those are there, and then make some decisions on how we would be able to handle some of these as well. Taking care of these, rather than just ignoring them, is going to make sure that we are able to get accurate and trustworthy results.

a. There are a few methods that we are able to use to make this work for our needs. For example, we may want to spend some of our time working on those outliers and deciding whether or not they are that important. If you look at a little graph about the information in your set of data, and you see there are quite a few outliers that seem to converge together in one general area, this is a good breakthrough to spend some time on. You should at least look into it to figure out if this is something that you should pay attention to and whether it is new information, like a new niche, that is important to you.

b. This doesn't mean that all of the outliers that you find are going to be important. Some of them may just be something strange that shows up in the information and if you leave it in there, it is going to end up messing with some of the results that you get along the way. This is why we have to double-check what we are seeing and make sure that it is matching up the way that we think it should, and then decide whether or not those outliers are important for us.

5. The next step that we need to spend some time on is creating our own Python algorithm with the help of machine learning. We have already spent some of our time taking a look at machine learning and all of the neat things that you are able to do with this. But in this step, we are going to use machine learning to help us read through the data after it has been trained and tested, and provide us with some of the insights and more that we need.

   a. There are going to be several algorithms that we are able to choose from when it is time to work with this kind of process, and we need to know more about our project, and all of the parts that come with it, in order to figure out what is going to be the best for us. Remember that we can't just pick out an algorithm and assume that it is going to work out the way that we want. We have to spend some time training, testing and making sure that the algorithm is going to work the way that we want.

6. Look over the patterns and insights that these algorithms are able to find in the data. One of the

main points that we will notice when we are handling this kind of data analysis is that it is going to help us take over a large amount of data and then look through it to find all of the important information that is inside of it. The more that we are able to spend our tying studying the data, and the stronger the algorithm that we choose, the easier it is to find the insights and all of the hidden and important values that are inside of it. Then we can use all of this information and the patterns that we are given t hep we make informed and better decisions overall.

7. Create a visualization: This is not a step that you should miss out on at all. These visuals are going to make it easier for those who are in charge of looking over the information to really see the connections and the relationships that show up in that data. This makes it easier for you to really figure out what the data is saying, and to figure out what decisions you should make based on that.

   a. There are a number of different types of visuals that you are able to work with, but the kind of data that you are sorting through, and the comparisons that you would like to make, are going to help you figure out the right one for your needs. Things like charts, graphs, and more will be the best options for helping you to get through this process as well.

As we can see, there are a lot of different parts that come with our data analysis and what we are able to do with this process. Taking the time to go through and learn more about the data analysis can make a big difference when it comes to how you will run your business. You will be able to use this in order to sort through all of the data you have collected and learned what is hidden inside. These can then be helpful when reaching out to your customers, working on marketing, figuring out how to open up a new niche to explore and more. But we first need to get ourselves through the process known as data analysis before we are able to use the data that we have been collecting.

As you can imagine from this already, there are going to be quite a few benefits that we are going to be able to see when it is time to work with data analysis. There are many times when you will need to work with this kind of analysis, because it is the part in the data science process that will allow you to finally take some of the data out of your set, and push it through the chosen algorithms, hopefully ones that have been tested and are ready to go

Chapter 9: The Importance of Data Visualizations to Finish the Process

While we are on this process, we need to spend some time taking a look at the importance of data visualizations and how this can help us to really see some of the results when it comes to our analysis. Sometimes, reading through all of the data that we have, and making it make sense to us is going to be hard when we have to look through a lot of different reports and documents. Sometimes, having this in the picture form, or in some kind of visual, is going to make a world of difference in the success that we have, and the ease of understanding the data that is being presented to you.

This is exactly the spot where we will see the data visualizations come into play. These visuals are going to be helpful because they are able to take all of the data that we were able to collect in the past, and all of the predictions and patterns that the algorithms of Python have been able to show us, and then will place it into a form that is really easy for us to see and understand.

When these visuals are done in the right manner, and usually with the help of a Python library like Matplotlib, we will find that they are a great way to see some of the complex relationships that are present inside of all that data that we have been trying to sort through for such a long time already. For most people, looking through the visuals, rather than just reading through the documents and forms that we have will be a lot easier overall.

The process of data visuals is going to be a presentation of the data so that it turns into a format that we are able to read through and understand better than before. The reason that we are going to work on this one is that it is going to really help us to see things clearly, without guessing or spending hours looking over things, and can help a company make better decisions.

With visuals that add in a bit of interaction with them, we are going to be able to take some of the benefits of this whole concept of visuals even further. What this means is that we are able to not just put a visual out there, but we can add in lots of different types of technologies in order to drill down into the charts and graphs in more details, which will help us to interactively change up the data when we want, such as making changes to the visuals when some more data is added into the mix. With this all laid out, it is time for us to look closer at the visuals that we have and gain a better understanding of how these are meant to work.

The first thing that we need to take a look at is going to be why these kinds of visuals are going to be so important in the first place. Since the brain is really good at processing out the information that we have in a certain manner, using charts and graphs, and basically any kind of picture or visual in order to help it understand how large amounts of data are going to relate to one another.

Yes, we can read through the information and learn from it. But this process is a whole lot slower than looking at a graph or a chart of this information. And it is likely that we are not going to retain that information as well either. Using the visuals along with some of the reports or the documents that we have is going to be one of the best ways to share that information and learn from it in the process.

Data visualization is a great process to add in with your data analysis. It is a quick and easy way to convey some of the concepts that we have in a universal manner. In addition, we are able to experiment with a lot of different scenarios on the visualization, making a few small adjustments to see what that will do with some of the information that you are working with and the results that you would get from that data.

There are a lot of things that the data visualization is going to be able to help you out with. Some of the ways that we can utilize this data visualization will include:

1. It can identify the areas that need the most improvement or your full attention.
2. Clarify which factors are going to be the most important when it comes to influencing the behavior of your customer.
3. It can help you to take some of your products and understand where you should place them in order to get the most sales.
4. It is a great tool to use to make it easier to predict sales volumes throughout different times of the year.

From here, we need to take a look at some of the ways that these data visualizations will be used. You will find that pretty much all industries are going to be able to benefit when it comes to these kinds of visuals. Many of them already now some of the value of collecting this data and that it is important to then analyze the data as well. But now many of them are taking it a bit further and looking at it from a more visual standpoint.

These visual forms are going to make it easier to learn the insights and the predictions that are in all of that data, and that the algorithms were able to find, compared to other options. Some of the ways that these visuals are going to come into play, no matter which industry you are working with, will include:

You can use these kinds of visuals to help make it easier to have a good comprehension of your information and what is found in it, more quickly. By working with a representation of a business that is going to be more graphical in nature, especially when it contains the information that the business has collected it is going to be easier for companies to look through a lot of data in a manner that is much easier and clearer for them to see. And these visuals are also going to be there to make it easier for those who make the big decisions in the company to draw out conclusions from that information.

In addition, it is going to be a lot faster when we are able to analyze information that is found in a more graphical format, compared to analyzing the information that is found in a report or in some kind of spreadsheet. This is in comparison to analyzing information that is found in some kind of report or a spreadsheet. This can also mean that it is easier for these companies to see large amounts of data in a clear and easier manner to understand, and can help the business to address some of the issues that they have, answer questions in a timely manner, and so much more.

One of the other benefits that we are going to be able to see when we work with these data visuals and another way that many companies are going to rely on these visuals is to help us identify some of the patterns and relationships that are going to show up in our data. Even when we are working with extensive amounts of data that seem to be really complicated, we are able to change this around and use the visuals in order to help us make more sense out of that data as well. In fact, when we work with these visuals, we will find that it is a lot easier for a business to handle any of the parameters that are going to be more highly correlated in the process.

One thing that we need to keep in mind with this one is that many times the correlations that we see in these visuals may be obvious, and we can find them and use them for our needs without needing to bring in a visual at all. But then there are going to be times when these correlations are not going to be as obvious, and this is when the visuals are going to be so important to help us figure out these trends. When a company is able to use these options in order to identify the important patterns and relationships, it is going to be a lot easier for them to really focus on the right areas and influence their goals in the best manner possible.

Data visualizations are also able to help a business to discover some trends in the market. Sometimes these trends are going to be just in the market, and other times they can be trends that are specific to the business. When the business is able to find these trends and use them for their advantage, then it is the perfect way to gain an edge over the competition. And this always leads to increasing the bottom line of that company, no matter what industry they are working with.

With the right kind of visualization in place, and with these visuals being used in the proper way, it is much easier to spot some of the outliers that show up in your data. And sometimes, these are the outliers that are going to affect the quality of the product or even the customer churn. You can also use this to address some of the potential issues that we have before they turn into some really big problems for the company.

In addition, it is possible to use this data visualization to help communicate a story to others. Once a business has been able to uncover some new insights with the help of these visuals, the next step that comes along is to communicate these insights to some others, whether it is the people who make the decisions in the business, the stakeholders, or someone else who is important to this process for your business.

When we are able to work with some of these visuals, whether we are looking at some of the graphs, charts, and other representations of data that are impactful, we know that this kind of work is going to be important when we are working with our data analysis. This is due to the fact that it will help us to keep engagement up some more and will help us to get the information shared and ready to go as quickly as possible.

Before we try to implement some of the new technology that we are looking at and talking about when it comes to data analysis, there are going to be a few important steps that we have to follow in the first place. Not only does a data scientist or a company that is using a data analysis need to have a good grasp on the data they are taking a look at, but they are also going to need to have a good grasp at what kind of data they are looking for, what goals they would like to have, and even their audience.

Being able to prepare the company for the technology that is going to come with these data visuals is going to require that we are able to get a few things in place first, and these will include:

1. The data scientist, to start off, is going to need to understand all of the data that they would like to be able to visualize. The most important thing that we are able to understand about the data including how unique the values of data in that column are, which is the cardinality, as well as the size of the data.

2. We also need to make sure that we are able to determine what we are working to visualize. We can't just use a random visual and assume that it is going to work with the right option. You can experiment with a few and try them out, but it is always a good option to work with in order to get familiar with the visuals that you are using to keep things organized and safe.

3. Another thing that we need to focus on here is that we must know a bit about our audience and have a good idea of how the audience is able to process the information in a manner that is more visual.

4. And finally, we need to take a look at using the visual in a manner that is able to take in all of the

information and all of the data, and then is able to convey the data in the best option in the easiest form to understand.

After we have had a chance to go through the four parts that are above, you will be able to answer the initial questions that you have about the types of data you want to work with and the audience who is most likely to consume the information. Then we can go through and prepare the data so that it is ready to go straight into the visual that we want to work with.

This is a lot of things to keep in check, and sometimes it is not going to work as well as we would hope. Be ready to take on more work and realize that this is a process that is not going to be as instant and you may have hoped in the beginning. But when it is all said and done, you will have some of the answers that you need. Plus, we will often find that this data can be generated faster than it can be analyzed and processed.

There are factors that we need to consider during this stage as well. This could include something like the cardinality of columns that you are looking to visualize. When we see that the cardinality is higher, this means that there are going to be a large number of unique values. Think about the account numbers at a bank for this one. If we see that the cardinality is low, it could mean that there are a lot of repeat values that show up in the information. This could happen when we work on a column that includes the gender of the person.

There are a lot of benefits that are going to come into play when it is time to work on a data visualization. This is going to be the best way for you to really showcase the information that you have and to make sure that it is in a form that is easy to understand and use all of the time.

You can certainly spend some time just working with just the reports and other options along the way to show off the information and the insights that you are able to get from all of that data and the algorithms that you want to use. But this doesn't help us to see the relationships and more that we need like we can with the visuals. And because there are so many different options that we are able to choose when it comes to the right visuals, you will find that you are certain to find the one that is right for your needs. When you are ready to really work with data analysis or a data science project, and you want to learn how the data is going to relate to one another, then you will need to work through data visualization to help make this happen.

Chapter 10: How Data Science Can Take Businesses into the Future

The final thing that we need to take a look at when it comes to the world of data science is some of the ways that this is able to help us reach the future. There are so many things to consider when it is time to work on our businesses and hope that we can be successful for a long time in the future. In the past, there was a lot of uncertainty that came with the future of a business and how it was going to work. But now we can use data science to help us to see some good results when it comes to our business and learning what decisions to make in the future.

We can quickly see that data science is going to be a great option to use in order to help your business be successful and see some of the benefits that you would like to see in the future. Some of the different things that we are able to see when it comes to the world of data science and all that it is able to do for our needs will include:

Helps You Learn More About Your Customers

One of the top ways that data science is going to be used is as a way to learn more about the customers you have around you. This can work well for marketing purposes, and even to help you figure out new ways to reach your customers and new niches that may be the right one for you. With such a diverse and varied and spread out customer base as most businesses have today, it is important to learn the best way to reach your customers, and exactly what they are looking for when they pick your business or one like you.

All businesses can benefit from learning more about their customers, and your business is not going to be any different along the way. You need to be open to some of the new ideas that are there, and even some of the new demographics that you may not have considered in the past. This is where some of the outliers are going to come into play.

If you see that there are a number of outliers that match up together away from the average, in the same spot, then this is a really good place to look at. It could tell you more about a new product, or even a new niche and demographic, that you should focus on in order to help grow your business. And if things go right, you may find that it is the right one to use, but also one you and the competition had never thought about before, making it the perfect way to reach your customers where they are, without having a bunch of competition there yet.

Of course, you will find that it can tell us some of the basics about the customers that you are working with as well. This can help us to work with the right customers, reach them right where they are, and ensure that we are going to be able to get to those customers in the way that we need to increase our sales. This is something that has always been a struggle for a lot of businesses, but with the help of some of the work in data analysis and data science, it is now something that we are able to do with a great deal of accuracy compared to the past.

Cut Out Fraud and Other Issues

Many of the financial companies out there are going to use data science in order to help them out in many aspects. Data science and some of the machine learning that goes with it that can cut out on some of the noise and really learn from the past data that is presented to it will be able to help out these industries when it comes to fraud and even helping with underwriting some of the loans out there.

Fraud is a big issue that comes up on a regular basis. And many of those who are going to steal credit card information and more and use it for their own personal gain are getting smarter with some of the options that they decide to use. It is not enough to just set up a maximum amount that the user can spend and say that will catch everything. But having someone watch all of the credit card transactions that are going through for a company would be overwhelming and not all that effective.

You will find though that with the help of some of the machine learning algorithms, we are able to feed in information about past transactions that we know are fraudulent and allow the algorithm to learn. The algorithm is then able to go through and pick out, from some of the new transactions that show up, which options are going to be fraudulent, which ones need to be checked by a human, and which ones are going to be safe. This can help save credit cards, banks, and other financial institutions billions a year.

Another way that many of these companies are going to start using data science in the future is to help them when picking out who to give loans to or not. This may seem a bit unfair and like it takes some of the personal touches out of the whole thing when a computer gets to decide. But these can help to cut down on the bad applications that are accepted and reduce the amount of waste that the bank or financial institution is taking on overall.

For the customer, this is going to result in some faster processing times. If you are accepted, you will find out much faster, and usually with a better interest rate, than what was happening in the past. So, while this may seem like something that is only going to benefit the lender, it is actually something that can benefit both parties.

Learn How to Cut Out Waste

All companies have some kind of waste. But it isn't always what you may think. Just because you are not throwing away countless boxes of paper or trash on a daily basis does not mean that you are not dealing with a lot of waste that is cutting into your profits and making you less competitive because you have to charge more of your products.

There could be a waste in how long a process takes. If you can find a faster method to use to create a product or service, one that keeps the same quality that the customer has come to expect, and does not cause harm to the employees in the process, then this is something that you need to consider looking into. And that is where data science can help.

Do you notice that there seems to be a lot of downtimes, or waiting time in between the different steps of the process? Or maybe there is a kind of bottleneck that is going to come up when we work on this process, and while everyone else is speeding up, one place is stopping it all and can't keep up, and the others after it are just waiting around? This is not an efficient use of your employees and machine to just have them standing around, and data science will be able to help you figure this out and make some of the changes that are necessary.

What about when one of the machines in your company ends up breaking down? This can often happen right in the middle of the day and then all operations have to stop and no employee can work, even though they are getting paid until it is fixed. Machine learning and data science are able to come into this and make predictions on when a part in the machine is going to break down, based on how often you use it and the age of the part. Then you can schedule the best time to fix that part, rather than trying to get it done at the worst times.

These are just a few of the places where we are likely to see a lot of waste when it comes to our business, no matter what kind of industry we are in. it is important to learn how to reduce this kind of waste, and more, as much as possible, so that we are able to see some good results in the process. When we reduce the waste, we reduce the cost that we experience, and this can make it a whole lot easier to keep prices down, remain competitive, and really see some of the results that we want in the process.

How to Handle Your Competition

In our modern world, there is always a lot of competition. In the past, the competition that you had to work against was usually those that were nearby. You didn't have to compete against anyone who was more than a short drive away because people would not go that far to get what they wanted. Now, with modern technology and the use of the internet, your competition could be on the other side of the world.

The ease of using the internet to set up your own shop is going to cause some of the problems as well. So many small businesses and at home businesses will start up in your industry as well, which means more types of competition that you have to fight against. And all of this is going to make it really hard to see some of the success that you would like unless you can find ways to distinguish yourself from all of the noise.

This is where the data science project is going to come in. You can use this to figure out some new ways to market to your customers and get them to choose you over someone else. You can use this in order to learn more about the other competitors and what they are doing that you could do better, or at least in a different manner, to beat them out. You can use data science to help you figure out a new niche to reach, help you to figure out which products you would like to sell, and so much more. Sometimes even just learning more about the industry that you are in can be a good goal when we are handling some of the work of data science.

Make Better Business Decisions

Many companies are choosing to go with data science, and all of the other steps that we have spent some time on in this guidebook, in order to help them make some smarter business decisions overall. In the past, there was always an element of risk that came with making some good business decisions. If you wanted to be able to pick out the next product that should sell or figure out which direction you had to take for your business, it was hard. There had to be a good mix of business smarts, knowledge of being in the industry for a long time, and a ton of risk to get it all to work.

Data science is able to change this. As long as you are able to use the process of data science in the proper manner, you will find that it is going to help you to reduce your risks, while also helping to make decisions that you are confident are the right ones for your needs. You will have all of the data, and a well-trained algorithm, to help you get this done, and will ensure that you are going to be able to make smart business decisions overall.

No longer will you need to worry about the amount of risk that comes with some of the decisions that you have to make. No longer will you need to focus on the pros and the cons of something. All of this is going to be done with the right project in data science, and with the help of good data and strong machine learning algorithms along the way. When you can combine these together, you will be able to get the assurance that you need that you are always making the best business decisions all the time.

Data science is really changing up every industry that it touches. Whether you are working in retail, the medical field, manufacturing, marketing, financial fields, or somewhere else, you will find that data science is able to help you do your work better. Your customers are going to notice, the competition is going to see that you are blowing right past them, and it won't be long before you are able to really see some improvements.

Right now, there is just a lot of speculation out there about how this data science is going to work and how far it can take us in the future. But seeing what it has been able to do so far, and how much it has been able to help out a lot of businesses overall, can really give us some hope for how great this is going to be in the future as well.

Conclusion

Thank you for reading *Python Data Science*. I hope that you enjoyed this book and found out the information that you need about how to work with Python along with your data science project today.

In this guidebook, we spent a lot of time taking a look at the process of data science, and why it has become so important to so many different businesses over time. it is a great process, one that allows a company to take in as much information as they can, and then learn some of the valuable insights and predictions that they need to help them run their business better.

As we discussed a bit more in this guidebook, the data that we are able to gather is not going to be as structured and easy to sort through as it was in the past. This is going to make it a bit harder for us to go through and actually sort through the data manually as we could in the past. It also means that because the data does not need to be organized to be available, we are able to find a lot more of this information overall as well.

But with all of this data and all of the organization that is missing from the data, it is a small wonder that we are able to learn anything out of the data at all. But this is exactly where data science is going to come into play and will help us to get started in no time. When we work with data science and all that it is going to provide to us along the way, we will learn that it is possible, through a series of steps like gathering the data, cleaning it, and sending it through the right algorithms, that will help us to learn more about what is found in the data and what we are able to do to make it work for our needs.

This guidebook took some time to explain more about what the data science process is all about. We explored data science and some of the basics of this language. We then worked with the process of Python and how this can work with the data science project to get the best results. From there we moved on to some of the benefits of data science, how to work with data mining, the importance of data cleaning and organizing and so much more.

This is not where the process is going to stop though. We also get to spend some time looking at the basics of machine learning, and how this ties into one particular step of data science, the data analysis. This is the fun step, where we get to work on training some of our models to make them work the way that we want and to ensure that we actually learn the right predictions and more from that data. We spent a good deal of time looking at these topics, along with the data analysis to make sure your information was ready to go.

The end of this guidebook will take look at what the importance of data visuals is all about, and some of the ways that we are likely to use data science and the machine learning process to help us get started on the right track. All of this is going to come together to help us create some of the best codes that we need to finally get the right results.

There are many books on this topic, and we hope this one provides you with the information and skills that you need to get the best results. If you found this guidebook helpful to you, make sure to leave a review!

Coding with Python

A Simple Guide to Start learning:
Lots of Exercises and Projects for
Distributed Computing Systems

Tim Wired

Introduction

Congratulations on purchasing *Coding with Python,* and thank you for doing so.

The following chapters will discuss all of the different parts that we need to know when we are ready to start coding in Python and seeing some of the results that we want as a beginner with our own codes. There may be some other options out there that you are able to choose when it comes to writing out codes and getting your programs and applications done, but you will quickly see that none of them are going to provide you with the options and the versatility that you are looking for like we can see with the Python coding language.

Inside this guidebook, we are going to spend some time looking at the Python language and all that it is able to provide for us when it is time to start our work with coding. You will find that while this is a simple language to work with, it will still provide you with all of the options and more that you are looking for overall. And we are going to explore a lot of these in this guidebook today!

To start with, we are going to spend some time taking a look at the basics of the Python language. We will find that we can learn about the benefits of this language, why you would want to work with this language, and so much more. Then we are going to move on to some of the basics that come with downloading and installing the Python language on your system, and some of the most basic parts that come with coding in this kind of language. This will help us to make sure that we are able to get all of the parts done that we are looking for and will ensure that we are able to get the results that we want.

From there, we can then move on to some of the other options of what we are able to do when it comes to the Python language. For example, we are going to find that we are able to work with things like creating our own classes and exploring some of the cool things that we are able to do when it comes to working with an OOP language. This is a really neat feature that comes with some of the more modern coding languages that are out there, and it is really important to helping us to get things done with some of the codings that we want to work with.

There are a lot of other things that we are able to work with when it comes to the Python language, and this guidebook is going to help us walk through this and see all of the really neat things that we are able to do within this kind of language. For example, we will take a look at how to work with the variables, the conditional statements, so the program is able to make some decisions on its own without the programming having to guess what input the user is going to rely on all of the time and more.

This is just the beginning of what we will be able to do with this kind of programming language though. We will also take a look at how we can focus on the loops to help us save some coding space and get the language to repeat the same line more than once. We can look at inheritances to see how we can reuse some of the previous parts of the code that we need to make our codes stronger and better than ever before. And we will even look at how to handle some of the exceptions that may show up in your coding to ensure that you are able to keep things organized and working the way that you would like along the way.

At the end of this guidebook, we are going to take a look at some of the simple tips and tricks that you are able to follow in order to get some of the best results that you would like out of the Python language. As a beginner, getting started on the right track will be able to help you get the most out of your coding needs. And this chapter will make sure that you are set up and ready to go when it is time to work on all of your codes.

All of these points are going to work together to help us to really see some great results when it comes to writing out our own codes. No matter what your goal is when it comes to writing out some of the codes that we need in Python, or for any other language, learning the basics and how we are able to use these for some of our needs are going to be so important. We are going to make sure that we go through these basics and learn some of the parts to help us really get things done in no time.

There may be quite a few coding languages out there that you are able to work with. But it is important for us to spend some time looking at the different parts that come with this coding language so that we are able to write out some of the codes that we want to use at this time as well. When you are ready to learn how to work with the Python coding language and see what this kind of language is able to do for your websites, programs, and applications, then make sure to read this guidebook to help you get started.

There are plenty of books on this subject on the market, thanks again for choosing this one! Every effort was made to ensure it is full of as much useful information as possible; please enjoy it!

Chapter 1: The Python Language

Welcome to the world of Python programming! There are a lot of different options that you are able to choose when it is time to do some of the codings that you would like. But we have to remember that out of all of these, one of the best options that will help you to get some of the coding done that you would like. This guidebook is going to take some time to look at the Python language and what you are able to do with it to get your results in no time at all.

The Python language is one of the easier of the languages to learn, which is good news for someone who is just getting started with coding. But don't let this fool you; it has all of the power, features, and more that you need in order to really push yourself forward and to help you see some amazing results with the coding that you would like to use. Let's take a look at the Python language and what we are able to do when it comes to using this language for all of your coding needs.

What is the Python Language?

In technical terms, you will find that Python is going to be a great coding language that we are able to work with when it is time to handle some of the codings that you would like to get done. This is going to be integrated with some of the dynamic semantics that is going to help with issues of app development and web development. It is going to be a field of Rapid Application Development because it is going to provide us with a way to work with dynamic typing and binding options.

One of the nice things that come with Python is that it is relatively simple, so it will be easy to learn. This is because it is going to require a unique syntax that focuses on readability, so it is easier to use. Developers will be able to translate and read the code of Python much easier than some of the other languages that are out there.

Thanks to this, we will see a reduction in the cost of program maintenance and development because it is going to allow the teams to work in a more collaborative manner, and there will not be any barriers that come with significant language and experiences like other options.

In addition, Python is going to support the use of modules and packages, which is going to mean that programs can be designed in a more modular style, and the code can be reused with more than one project at a time. once you have been able to develop a module or a package that you need, it can be scaled to be used in all of the projects out there, and it is easy to export these modules.

One of the most promising benefits that come with Python is that both the standard library as well as the interpreter are going to be available for us to use for free, in both the source and the binary form, based on what you would like to work with. Here is not going to be any kind of exclusivity either, because Python and all of the necessary tools that are going to be available on all of the major platforms. This means that Python can really be an enticing option to work with for developers who do not want to worry about some of the higher costs that work with development like other options do.

We can then take a look at some of the basics that come with Python. Python is going to be a general-purpose programming language, which is going to be another way to say that we are able to work with nearly everything. Most importantly, it is going to be known as an interpreted language, which means that the code that you are writing out is not going to be translated over to a format that is computer-readable when it is time to run through it.

While most of the languages for programming are going to do this conversion before the program can even run, this is not something that Python is going to work with. This type of language is going to be known as a scripting language because, in the beginning, it was more about helping you to work on some beginner projects. But over time, you will find that it is going to be expandable to some of the other projects that you would like to work with as well.

The concept of these kinds of scripting languages has changed quite a bit since it began. This is because Python is going to be used in a lot of different situations, such as to help us to write out large and commercial style applications rather than just some small and banal ones. This reliance on Python has grown more and more as we see more reliance and use on the internet.

We will also find that a large majority of web applications and a lot of different platforms out there are going to rely on Python, including the search engine of Google, YouTube, and some of the transactions that happen on the New York Stock Exchange that are based online. You know that when a system is able to handle some of these major things, that it is going to be a serious language that is going to help you to get a lot done.

As we can see, there are a lot of different parts that are going to happen when it is time to work with the Python programming language. There are a lot of different parts that come with the Python language, and learning how to make it work for our needs is going to make sure that we are going to be able to write out some of the programs that we would like as well.

The Benefits of Python

There are actually going to be a lot of different benefits that we are able to look at when it is time to handle some of your coding needs with the help of the Python coding language. In fact, this is often one of the most popular coding languages out there because there are so many options that we need to work with and so many benefits that come with this language. For someone who is just starting out and is not sure which kind of coding language to go with, you will find that Python is one of the best options to work with in order to really see some results in no time. Let's take a look at some of the benefits of the Python language, even if you are brand new to the world of coding overall.

To start with, Python is a language that has been designed to help a beginner out with some of their coding needs. If you are not certain about how to get started with some of the coding that you would like, and you want to get started, then Python is going to be one of the best options that you are able to work with overall. It was designed to make coding more accessible to those who have never done any coding in the past, with easy syntax and English as the primary language that comes with this.

If you have been worried about working with the Python language, and you want to ensure that you are actually able to handle some of the codes that you want, whether it is a simple code or a more complicated option, you will find that the Python language is going to be one of the best options to work with overall.

The good news here is that the Python language, even though it has been designed with a beginner in mind, it is still going to be one of the best options for you to use when it comes to power and strength that you need to get things done. You can work with machine learning, data science, and more all with this kind of language, which is going to really help you to see some of the results that you are looking for when it comes to seeing the most out of your own coding, even when you are a beginner.

Along with this same note, you will find that the Python language is going to come with a lot of support libraries to work with, as well. It is not going to take you a lot of time or research to figure out that the Python language has a ton of libraries and extensions that can work along with it. Depending on what you would like to do with some of your coding, you will find that you can get the library or the extension that you need, including with machine learning, math, science, data science, and more.

This is going to provide the beginner with a ton of help when they are first getting started with a language, and it is really going to make things easier when you get to coding. You will be able to also find more functions, classes, objects, and more when you decide to add in some of these parts to the process as well. You can also add in these libraries to make sure that you have the power and the functionality that you need along the way too.

Integration features: Python can be great because it integrates what is known as the Enterprise Application Integration. This really helps with a lot of the different things you want to work on in Python, including COBRA, COM, and more. It also has some powerful control capabilities as it calls directly through Java, C++, and C. Python also has the ability to process XML and other markup languages because it can run all of the modern operating systems, including Windows, Mac OS X, and Linux through the same kind of byte code.

The next benefit that we are going to see is that this language is going to add in some more of the productivity that the programmer gets to enjoy. The Python language is going to have a lot of designs with it that is more object-oriented, and this also allows it to work with a ton of support libraries. Because of these resources, and how easy it is to use the program, it is possible for the programmer to get more done and increase the amount of productivity that they are able to see.

Another great benefit that is going to come with this is that the Python language is going to really have a great community of other coders and developers to work with. Since Python is considered one of the most popular coding languages out there, this means that you are going to find a ton of communities out there that you are able to use to help you get better with programming.

When you work on some of your own codes, you will find that sometimes things are not going to match up the way that you would like, or you end up with some troubleshooting that you just can't figure out. Or maybe you just want to learn something new and need help getting it done. That is where these communities are going to come into play. You can visit these communities to ask questions, to get some help, and even learn something new along the way.

And finally, we are going to take a look at how the Python code is going to be open-sourced. This may not mean all that much right now, but it does mean that we will be able to use the code for free and make the changes and modifications that we need in order to really get our codes to run properly. It also means that you can easily download and use the original Python in any manner that you would like.

Of course, there are some companies that may have taken Python and added some additional features and more to help out with Python. And if you choose to work with some of these, you may need to spend a bit of money to download and use them. But it is completely possible that you can get started with some of the programming that you want to do in Python all for free and without having to worry about having to deal with the copyright.

There are a lot of things to enjoy when it comes to working with the Python language, and we have just gotten started with this list. As you will quickly see through this process, and as we go through some more of the steps that are needed in this guidebook, it is going to be a lot easier to see some more of these benefits as we go through the coding as well.

The Python Interpreter

When we are taking a look at the standard installation that is found with Python, and when we are able to work with the version that is found on www.python.org, you will find that there are a lot of files that are found with this. It is going to contain documentation, the information that you need licensing, and some of the files that you need to develop the codes that you would like. These are going to include the Shell, IDLE, and the interpreter.

The first thing that we are going to spend our time here is the Python interpreter. This is going to be responsible because it is responsible for helping us to execute any of the scripts that we want to write. The interpreter is able to take all of the script files that you write out in this and turns them into instructions. Then it will go through and write them out based on the codes that you would like to work with as well.

While we are here, we also need to take a look at the part that is known as the Python IDLE. This is going to be known as the Integrated Development and Learning Environment. And it is important because it will hold onto all of the other tools that you need to help make developing all of the programs that you want in Python as easy as possible. Depending on which version of Python that you are working with, the IDLE can also be extensive, or it can be a bit easier to work with as well.

If you don't like the version that is on with Python when you download it, there are often other methods and versions that you can choose to download, as well. And at the same time, you are able to find a new text editor to handle some of the work that you are doing. This is something that is important when you want to make sure that you get specific features to help you get your work done, as well. But the traditional form of the IDLE and text editors that come with the original download of Python will really help you to get some of the work done that you would like.

We also have to make sure that we are working with a good Python Shell along the way. This is going to be an interactive command-line driven interface that is going to be found in the interpreter that you work with. This will hold onto some of the commands that you will want to write out. if the shell is able to understand what you are writing out, then it is going to be helpful at going through and executing all of the code that you want to write. But if something goes wrong and it doesn't understand the code, or you are not able to write it out in the proper manner, then you will end up with an error message showing up on the system instead.

All of these different parts are going to be important when you would like to write out some of the codes that you have in Python. When you are working with the installation of this language through the website above, all of these parts are automatically going to be installed on your system for you, and this makes it easy without any additional steps to be taken. But if you decide to go through and get the version of Python that you want to use from another location, check out to see whether these are going to contain everything that you need or not before you try to work with your own coding.

Chapter 2: How to Install Python On Your Computer

Now that we know a bit more about the Python language and what all it is able to do, it is time for us to learn how we are able to install the Python language on our system. The good news here is that this language is going to be able to provide us with a lot of easy steps to get the files we need to be downloaded on any computer that we want, regardless of the operating system that is found there. This means that regardless of whether you are going to work with Windows, Linux, or Mac, you will be able to make this all work and can start using the Python language in no time.

While we are going to take a look at how to get going with the installation process of Python on all three of the major operating systems in a moment, we are going to bring up a few ideas ahead of time. First, we need to make sure that we have an IDE with this, and usually a text editor as well. This will ensure that we are able to actually write the codes. So, no matter where we get the Python file from, we have to make sure that it is going to have the right files so that you can actually write out the codes that you want.

For our purposes here, we are going to spend some time looking at installing the Python language from the website www.python.org. This is the original website that comes with the Python language and will provide you with a free version of Python. You will also be assured that when you download this website, you will then be able to go through and have all of the files that are needed to get started with this all in one place.

Keep in mind when you work with the Python language, and you decide to work with a third-party website to download this, make sure that it has all of the files that you need ahead of time. this will make it easier for you to get started with the coding right after the installation is done. Keep in mind also that when you install some of these third-party versions, they may cost a bit to get started.

With this in mind, let's take a look at some of the steps that you are able to use in order to get the Python language, and all of the files that you need, on any operating system that you would like.

Installing Python

The first operating system that we are going to take a look at is how to install the Python language on a Mac operating system. The good news is that with this operating system, there is usually some version of Python 2 already preinstalled on the system. The exact version of this Python that you would like to work with is going to depend on which version of this operating system that is on your system. If you would like to figure out which one is there, open up your terminal app on the Mac and type in the code below:

Python – V

This is also going to show you some kind of number so that you can see which version of Python is there. you are also able to choose to install the Python 3 on the system if you would like, and it isn't going to be necessary to go through and uninstall this as you go through it, even if you do upload the Python 3 version of your choice. First, we need to make sure that we will not have one of these versions on your computer already or not. The coding that we will be able to use with this one will include:

Python3 – V

The default on OS X is that Python 3 is not going to be installed at all. If you want to use Python 3, you can install it using some of the installers that are on Python.org. This is a good place to go because it will install everything that you need to write and execute your codes with Python. It will have the Python shell, the IDLE development tools, and the interpreter. Unlike what happens with Python 2.X, these tools are installed as a standard application in the Applications folder.

Another option that we are able to spend some time on and work with is going to be the Windows system. This one is going to be a bit different than what we will see with the Mac operating system, but it is still something good that we are able to work with as well. You will find though that this one will not automatically have a version of Python on it at all unless you actually got the computer from someone who did it ahead of time for you.

This is because Microsoft has come up with their own programming language, and this is why we are going to see that the Python language is not going to be present on these systems. The good news is that you can still install Python on your system, and it is going to work just fine for your needs. It just takes a few more steps to get it all done than you would see with some of the other options. The steps that we need to work within order to get the Python language to work on a Windows operating system will include:

1. To set this up, you need to visit the official Python download page and grab the Windows installer. You can choose to do the latest version of Python 3, or go with another option. By default, the installer is going to provide you with the 32-bit version of Python, but you can choose to switch this to the 64-bit version if you wish. The 32-bit is often best to make sure that there aren't any compatibility issues with the older packages, but you can experiment if you wish.

2. Now right-click on the installer and select "Run as Administrator." There are going to be two options to choose from. You will want to pick out "Customize Installation"

3. On the following screen, make sure all of the boxes under "Optional Features" are clicked and then click to move on.

4. While under Advanced Options" you should pick out the location where you want Python to be

installed. Click on Install. Give it some time to finish and then close the installer.

5. Next, set the PATH variable for the system so that it includes directories that will include packages and other components that you will need later. To do this, use the following instructions:

   a. Open up the Control Panel. Do this by clicking on the taskbar and typing in Control Panel. Click on the icon.

   b. Inside the Control Panel, search for Environment. Then click on Edit the System Environment Variables. From here, you can click on the button for Environment Variables.

   c. Go to the section for User Variables. You can either edit the PATH variable that is there, or you can create one.

   d. If there isn't a variable for PATH on the system, then create one by clicking on New. Make the name for the PATH variable and add it to the directories that you want. Click on close all the control Panel dialogs and move on.

6. Now you can open up your command prompt. Do this by clicking on Start Menu, then Windows System, and then Command Prompt. Type in "python." This is going to load up the Python interpreter for you.

Don't let all of these steps scare you as you go through this process. It is actually quite a bit easier to work with than it looks, and in no time at all, you will be able to create a program that works well and does what you would like. Once you are done working through the steps above, the Python language will be up and running on your computer, and ready to go for all of your needs, even on the Windows operating system.

And finally, we are going to take a look at some of the steps that you can take in order to get the Python language set up and ready to go on your operating system in no time. The first step that we are going to do with Linux, similar to what we did with the Mac operating system, is to check whether or not Python 3 is found on your system. You are then supposed to open up the command prompt in this operating system and use the code below to help you get started:

$ python3 - - version

If you are on Ubuntu 16.10 or newer, then it is a simple process to install Python 3.6. you just need to use the following commands:

$ sudo apt-get update
$ sudo apt-get install Python3.6

If you are relying on an older version of Ubuntu or another version, then you may want to work with the deadsnakes PPA, or another tool, to help you download the Python 3.6 version. The code that you need to do this includes:

```
$ sudo apt-get install software-properties-common
$ sudo add-apt repository ppa:deadsnakes/ppa
# sudo apt-get update
$ sudo apt-get install python3.6
```

The good news with this is that if you have worked with some of the other distributions of Linux in the past, then you should already have a version of Python 3 installed on your system. If you have not gone through and worked with some of the other distributions of Python before, then you will need to go through and add this onto your computer. You can even go through and install a more recent version of Python on the computer when you need it.

Chapter 3: The Important Basics to Writing Any Code in Python

Before we dive into some of the more complicated codes and methods that we are able to do with the Python language, it is time for us to spend some time learning the basics. These will ensure that we are set up for some of the more complicated options later on, and will ensure that we are going to see the best results later on with our coding. Some of the most important coding basics that we need to know in Python will include:

The Python Keywords

The Python keywords are going to be important because they allow us to take charge and provide some of the commands that we need inside of our code. These are reserved options and words in the language, ones that should only be used in order to tell the compiler the commands that you would like for it to follow. There are quite a few of these that are going to show up in the Python language, but if we are not careful and we don't use it in the proper way, the compiler will get confused and will run an error message for us. Remember what the keywords in Python are, and then just use them in the right place as the commands that you need.

How to Write a Comment

```
#!/usr/bin/env python
" " "

Docstring

" " "
# Comment
myvar="String"
```

We can't get too far in our discussion of the basics of Python without taking a look at the comments that are there and what we are able to do with these. If you are writing out some of the codes that you want to use, there are times when you will want to leave a note or a message inside of the code, letting others know what you are doing in the code or why one part is important. But you want to make sure that you are adding these without ruining the code and not getting it to work.

We are able to do all of this with the help of the comments. In Python, we will work with the # symbol to let the compiler know that we want to add in a comment at that point, and then the compiler will know to skip right over that part without concentrating on it or stopping at it at all. This makes it easier to add in as many of these comments as you would like. But it is often best to keep the number of these down to a minimum to help make sure that your code is as nice and organized as possible.

The Importance of the Variables

Variables are another part of the code that you will need to know about because they are so common in your code. The variables are there to help store some of the values that you place in the code, helping them to stay organized and nice. You can easily add in some of the values to the right variable simply by using the equal sign. It is even possible for you to take two values and add them to the same variables if you want, and you will see this occur in a few of the codes that we discuss through this guidebook. Variables are very common, and you will easily see them throughout the examples that we show.

Why Focus on the Classes?

When we work with the Python code, you will quickly find that the classes are going to be important when we are working with our codes. These classes are going to be the basic organizational structure that comes with Python and other OOP languages and will ensure that all of the different items in our codes, or the objects, are going to be organized and will come up when we need them

As we go through this guidebook, you will see that we do spend some time talking about classes and how we are able to organize them to make as much sense as possible. But there are a lot of benefits that come with these classes and being able to make them work for our needs, and creating them in a manner that will hold onto the objects that we have, is going to be very important.

Naming Your Identifiers

Your identifiers can be important to your code as well, and in Python, there are quite a few identifiers to work with too. You will find that they come in at a lot of different names, and you may seem them as functions, entities, variables, and classes. When you are naming an identifier, you can use the same information and the same rules will apply for each of them, which makes it easier for you to remember the rules.

The first rule to remember is when you name these identifiers. You have many options when you are naming your identifiers. For example, you can rely on both uppercase and lowercase letters with naming, as well as any number and the underscore symbol. You can also combine any of these together. One thing to remember here is that you can't start the name with a number, and there shouldn't be any spaces between the words that you write out. So, you can't write out 3words as a name, but you can write out words3 or threewords. Make sure that you don't use one of the keywords that we discussed above or you will end up with an error.

A Look at the Operators

The operators are a simple idea that we are able to work with when it comes to handling stuff in the Python language. These are simple, but they do help to add in some of the focus and power that we need in order to get more done when we are in this language. There are a number o different operators that we are able to focus on in the codes, so you are able to choose the one that is best for your needs.

For example, you can work with the arithmetic operators to help you finish some of the mathematical equations that you would like. You can work with the comparison operators to make sure that it is going to work to compare more than one part of the code together. And we can work with the assignment operators to ensure that we are able to assign the right value to the variable that we need along the way.

These are just a few of the basics that we will need when it is time to work with the Python language and get it up and running. As you go through this guidebook more and more over time, you will see a lot of these basics show up, and then you will feel more confidence over the work that you have been able to do. Make sure to study these a bit more and learn just why they are important to some of the coding that we are going to do here.

Chapter 4: Python As An OOP Language and How to Start Writing Your Own Classes

As we go through and look at some of the things that come with an OOP, or object-oriented programming, languages. Python is considered one of these kinds of languages and will help us to make codes a lot easier to work with. These types of languages will work with classes and objects that are pretty easy to manipulate, as well. These language types are going to work with the idea of classes and objects so that you can keep the code as organized as possible and can help you to get things done.

One of the features that you are going to enjoy when it comes to working with an OOP language is that the procedure that comes with any object that you use is going to come with some power to help access the fields of data, and in some cases, these objects can come in and make some modifications. When we look at an OOP language, you are able to design the program in the manner that you would like, simply by using a series of objects up and then getting them to interact with one another.

This may seem like a simplistic view to take of things, and if you have been a bit worried about doing anything in coding because of some of the challenges that are there, you may feel that taking this approach is going to leave you missing something. Or you may worry that the Python language is not going to have the power that you need to get the work done based on your programming needs.

You will quickly see that the OOP languages are important, and they can really add in a lot of the diversity that is needed for some of your codings. Each language is going to come with some languages, but the ones that you are likely to use, including the Python language, is going to be based on classes. What this means is that the code is going to have each of our objects belong to a class, which can help us to keep things organized, and will give us the freedom to know which objects we will need to work with.

As you work through Python, you will quickly find that an OOP language can make programming and code writing easier. If you ever spent time working with some of the older coding languages, you will notice that those older ones are much harder to work with and that OOP can make things easier. With the older coding languages, it's possible for your objects and other parts of the code to move around or end up in a different location than you had meant, which can make it hard to write the code and even debug it. But with an OOP language, you won't run into this problem because of the way that things are organized.

Before we go further into OOP languages and what they mean, we need to do a quick summary of classes and how they work. Classes are like small containers. You can pick any name that you want for the classes and then add in any item that you would like. Of course, to keep things organized and to help you call up these classes later on in your code, it may be a good idea to pick out a name that describes what is held inside.

When you decide that it is a good idea to work with these various objects that are in the code, you will find that these work the best because they can match up with actual items outside of the program. For example, you can work with an object that is a car, or one that is a book and then a third that is a ball. You also get the option of being able to pick out an object that is a bit more abstract, though this does add in another level of complexity to what we see as well. But we may find that this is going to help us get the right things done inside of our coding

These objects are going to be useful because they will stay inside any of the various classes that you create. You will be able to look at these classes simply as the containers that are able to hold onto the information that is found in your objects or to organize the objects that you have. you want to make sure though that when you place some objects into a newly created class that you make, that these objects are going to have some kind of similarities with each other, and that they make sense for being in the same class.

This doesn't mean that we are going to have to have only identical objects together in order to make this happen. But if you find that someone else looks into one of your classes, you will find that they can look at the code and will have a good idea of why you grouped together all of the objects that are inside of that particular class.

An example that we are going to be able to see with this is a class that you created for dogs. You do not have to just add in St Bernard's or just one type of dog to that class. You are able to include big dogs, small dogs, and any kind of dog in between. Any dog that you are able to think about or gather up can be added to this class about dogs. Other programmers are going to be able to see that these objects are not identical to one another, but they will understand that these are all dogs, so they belong in the same class as one another.

These objects and classes are going to be able to work with one another because they can help to make sure that your Python code stays as organized as you possibly can. You can spend some time learning how to put these objects in with the right class along the way, and we can look at some of the codes to help with this along the way. even as a beginner, you will be able to notice how much easier this coding can be when you work on these classes and objects.

Some of the Features of OOP Languages

The nice thing about working with the Python language is that it is considered an OOP language. And this will allow you the option to include a lot of the features and more that these kinds of languages will provide to us. The OOP language is going to rely on the objects and their classes to get this to work. But there are also going to be some other techniques and structures that are associated with the objects that are supported in Python. These are going to be important to help us learn more about and can help us to see how these languages will work. Some of the features that we can enjoy when it comes to the OOP language will include the following:

· Shared features from non-OOP languages: These languages may still have some features of low-level features from some of the older coding languages. Some of the examples of the features that are often still available in OOP languages include:

  • Variables: These variables are able to store your formatted information inside a few different data types. These are built-in to your languages, such as integers and characters. Variables can include things like hash tables, string, and lists.

  • Procedures: These can go by different names such as subroutines, routines, functions, and methods. They are going to take your input and then generate an output that you can then use for manipulating your data. The newer languages will have more structured concepts like loops and conditionals, which are both used a lot in Python.

- Classes and objects: We already spent some time talking about these through this chapter and will bring them up again later on. The classes are simply the containers that are able to hold onto your objects, no matter what kind of object you are working with. This helps you to call up those objects, or parts of the code, later on when needed.

- Dynamic dispatch and message passing: As you write some of your own codes, you will find that the external code is not the one that is responsible for selecting the procedural code that the method call will execute. This kind of responsibility is going to the object. The object will do this by looking at the method that is associated with that object during run time in a process that is known as dynamic dispatch. It helps to make sure that all parts of the code work well together and that you don't run into any issues.

- Encapsulation: This is a great feature that comes with the OOP languages. This is going to be a process that is going to help us to bind some of the data that we have. Any of the functions that we will see used for this process are going to be brought in to help manipulate the data and can help us to secure it from being misused in this code.

  - With the process that comes with encapsulation, we will get the benefit of knowing that when we call up the code, some other part is not going to be able to grab onto the code and make it go wrong. This will be one of the best ways to make sure that we are able to keep all of the objects in their right classes and to make sure that issues are avoided later on.

- Inheritances: We are going to take a look at how some of these inheritances are going to work a little bit later on. But any of the objects that you have should be able to hold, at a minimum one, but often more objects inside of them. When this does happen, we are going to call it the process of object composition. OOP languages are going to also be able to support a process known as inheritances, which means that we are able to create a new part of the code with the features and more that comes with the parent code from before.

- Open recursion: Along with some of the features that are found above with the OOP languages, you may find that some languages are going to support the open recursion option. This is where we are able to call over the object method and place it over to another method. You will just need to make sure that you use the keywords of self and this in order to get the process going. These variables are going to be known as late-bound, which means that they are going to allow the method that is defined in a class to invoke that method and then define it later on with some of your subclasses.

Of course, these are just a few of the great features that you will be able to use when it is time to work with an OOP language. As you go through this guidebook, you will soon see that there are a ton of features that come with these OOP languages and can help you to make sure that you are getting more out of your coding experience.

Coding Your Own Classes

Now that we have had some time to talk about the different things that you can do with objects and classes, it is time for us to go through and learn a bit more about how we are able to create some of our own classes, and how to make this whole process work. When we are coding in Python, we will spend some more time working on creating your own classes because it is going to help keep the code organized and will ensure that nothing will get lost along the way.

To help us to make one of these classes, though, you need to use the right keywords before we name the class. You can name the class anything that you would like in this process; we just have to make sure that the name is going to show up right after the keyword and that it is something that you are actually able to remember and hold onto later on.

Once you have had some time to name the class, it is then time to name a subclass, which is going to be placed inside of the parenthesis to stick with the proper rules of programming. Make sure that when you are near the end of the first line when you do create a class, that you have added in the semicolon to finish this off. While this is not something that is technically needed with some of the newer versions of Python and you can work the code if you forget to work with this part, it is still something that you should get done.

Writing out a class is going to sound more complicated at this point than it seems, so let's stop here and look at a good example of how you would be able to write out all of this in Python. Then we are going to be able to dive into a discussion as to what all of these parts mean, and why we are going to work with all of this as well:

```
class Vehicle(object):
#constructor
def_init_(self, steering, wheels, clutch, breaks, gears):
self._steering = steering
self._wheels = wheels
self._clutch = clutch
self._breaks =breaks
self._gears = gears
#destructor
def_del_(self):
 print("This is destructor....")
```

```
#member functions or methods
def Display_Vehicle(self):
print('Steering:' , self._steering)
print('Wheels:', self._wheels)
print('Clutch:', self._clutch)
print('Breaks:', self._breaks)
print('Gears:', self._gears)
#instantiate a vehicle option
myGenericVehicle = Vehicle('Power Steering', 4, 'Super
Clutch', 'Disk Breaks', 5)


myGenericVehicle.Display_Vehicle()
```

If you would like, you can try out this code. Just open up your text editor and type the code inside. As you work on writing this out, you will notice that a few of the topics we have already discussed in this guidebook show up in this code. Once you have a chance to write out and then execute this code, let's divide it up and see what happened above.

One of the first things that we need to take a look at here when we are trying to set up some of our classes is the class definition. This is going to be where you will need o to instantiate the object, and then you will be able to get the definition of the class. The reason that we want to work with this is that it will ensure that we are always picking out the right syntax that we want to work within the code.

This is something that we need to pay some special attention to because it is going to be where we tell the compiler what we would like to see it do. And it is able to highlight the commands that we think are the most important. If you would like to bring out a new definition of the class, you are able to work with the right functions, either the object_method) or the object_attribute.

Then we can move on to some of the special attributes here. These are going to be found in a lot of the codes that we want to work with, so they are important in helping us see results. These special attributes are going to be good because they can provide a programmer with some peace of mind because you can take the right steps to ensure that these special attributes are going to not get messed up and will be used in the proper manner.

When you look through some of the codings above, you will find that there are already a few examples of the special attributes that you are able to work with. Some of the other options that you are able to work with here will include the following:

__bases__: this is considered a tuple that contains any of the superclasses

__module__: this is where you are going to find the name of the module, and it will also hold your classes.

__name__: this will hold on to the class name.

__doc__: this is where you are going to find the reference string inside the document for your class.

__dict__: this is going to be the variable for the dict. Inside the class name.

The last thing that we are going to take a look at here is how to access members of the class hat we have created. We want to make sure that when we write out certain codes for our needs that the compiler and the text editor have a way to recognize the classes that we are creating. This is going to make it easier to execute the code in a proper manner.

Before we can make this happen, though, we have to make sure that the code is set up in the proper manner. As you go through with accessing the class, you will find that there are going to be a few methods that we are able to use to make this work. All of them are going to have their own special times when you will use them, and all of them are going to do their job well. But the number one method that a lot of programmers are going to focus on here because it is efficient and more is the accessor method.

To show us some of the ways that we are able to work with the accessor method, and to help us understand some of this and how it will work with a class that we already created we need to first take a look at some of the coding that is below:

```
class Cat(object)
itsAge = None
itsWeight = None
itsName = None
#set accessor function use to assign values to the fields or
member vars
def setItsAge(self, itsAge):
self.itsAge = itsAge

def setItsWeight(self, itsWeight):
self.itsWeight = itsWeight

def setItsName(self, itsName):
self.itsName =itsName

#get accessor function use to return the values from a field
def getItsAge(self):
return self.itsAge
def getItsWeight(self):
return self.itsWeight
```

```
def getItsName(self):
return self.itsName

objFrisky = Cat()
objFrisky.setItsAge(5)
objFrisky.setItsWeight(10)
objFrisky.setItsName("Frisky")
print("Cats Name is:", objFrisky.getItsname())
print("Its age is:", objFrisky.getItsAge())
print("Its weight is:", objFrisky.getItsName())
```

Before we move on, type this into your compiler. If you have your compiler run this, you are going to get some results that show up on the screen right away. This will include that the cat's name is Frisky (or you can change the name to something else if you want), that the age is 5, and that the weight is 10. This is the information that was put into the code, so the compiler is going to pull them up to give you the results that you want. You can take some time to add different options into the code and see how it changes over time.

There are a lot of times when you will find that classes are going to be easy to work with. These classes are going to be a good option to help us take care of some of the information we have and can make it easier to take care of the different objects that are going to show up in our code as well. Both the classes and the objects are things that we need to spend some of our time on here because they ensure that the code is going to be organized and that we are going to keep things set up the way that we would like along the way.

Chapter 5: Working with the Python Namespaces

Another option or topic that we need to spend some time on when it is time to work with the Python language is the idea of the namespace. Think about how many conflicts in names that happen all of the time in real life. When we think back to our lives in school, how many times were you in a class hat had two or more students that shared the same first name? If someone went into that class and asked for one of those students who had the same name, everyone would wonder which one they wanted because there are two people by the same name.

Now, usually, this could be solved with having the last name attached to the first name. this is another layer to the process that will ensure that we got ahold of the person who we wanted, even if they did share the same name with someone else. While it would be nice if this were not an issue, we can't assume that everyone in the world is going to give their child a different name.

All of this confusion and the process of being able to figure out the exact person we would like to bring up, and looking for other information outside of the first name could be avoided if we found a unique name for each person. This may not be such a big problem when you are working with a small class of about twenty students. However, it is going to be really hard to come up with a unique name when you are dealing with hundreds, and maybe even thousands, of people. And the issue becomes even harder when we are talking about the whole world.

Another issue in providing each child in the world with a unique name is that we have to work with the process of determining if someone else also has their name, but used a different spelling. We could have a Macey, Macie, Maci, and Macy. These are all the same names, but they look unique, and it can be really hard to make sure that we keep it organized and more.

Then there is a similar kind of conflict that we are going to see when we are working with programming. When you are going through and writing out a program that is small, such as one that just has 30 lines and no dependencies outside of the program, it is pretty easy for us to go through and provide it with some meaningful and unique names for all of the variables.

But the same kinds of issues are going to happen when the code gets longer. When there are thousands of lines of code found in your program, and you add in some of the external modules that you need, this is going to become even more complicated along the way. and this is why we will find that working with namespaces is going to be one of the best options to work with.

What are These Namespaces?

So, to dive into this a bit more, we need to learn more about what a namespace is all about. This is basically going to be a system that will make sure that all of the names found in a program are unique and that we are able to use these without any conflicts along the way. you might already know that a lot of the things that show up in Python, such as the functions, lists, and strings, will be an object. Another thing that is interesting here is that Python is going to implement these namespaces as a dictionary.

There is going to be a process that is known as name to object mapping, with the names as the keys and the objects more as the values. There is the possibility to work with multiple namespaces, and this means that we are able to use the same name and map it to a different object. There are a few examples that come with these namespaces including:

1. Local namespace: This is going to be a namespace of local names that are inside of the function. This namespace is created when a function is called, and it is only going to last until the function returns.

2. Global namespace: This namespace includes names from a lot of modules that are imported that you will use with your project. It is going to be created when we have a module created in our project, and it is going to last until the script is able to end.

3. Built-in namespace: This namespace is going to including the function and exception names that are built-in to our code.

What is the Scope?

The namespaces are going to help us out a lot with this because it is going to uniquely identify the names that are going to be showing up in our program. However, this isn't going to imply that we are allowed to work with the name of a variable anywhere that we would like. A name also is going to come with a scope that is able to define the program parts where you are able to work with the name, without having to add in any of the prefixes that we think need to be there.

Just like what we are going to see with the namespaces above, there is the potential for multiple scopes to show up in the program. Some of the options that you will have when it comes to scopes that are available when you execute a program will include:

1. A local scope. This one is going to be considered the innermost scope that is going to contain a list of all the local names that we are able to use in our current function.
2. A scope that is for all of the enclosing functions. The search for a name is going to be able to start, in this situation, from the nearest enclosing scope and then will move out.
3. A module-level scope. This is going to be the one that will contain all of the global names from the module that we are currently in.
4. The outermost scope is also important here because it is going to be the one that will contain a list of all the names that are built-in. This scope is going to be searched last in order to find the name that you referenced at the time.

Working with the namespaces and more in the proper manner is going to be important when it comes to working with this kind of process it will ensure that your code is going to work in the manner that you would like and that when you call up a variable or another part of the code, it is going to work in the manner that you would like and that the code is going to behave and know what you would like to have to pull up. It may not seem like it is that important to learn, but it can definitely make a difference in the kinds of codes that you are going to write along the way.

Chapter 6: The Decision Control Statements

It is also possible to spend some time working with what is known as decision control statements. These are going to be important in helping you take some of the codes that you have and turn them into something that is going to be strong and will accomplish the work that you want. Plus, they will be able to help the compiler make some good decisions, without having to worry about whether you can guess all of the answers that are there or not.

As a programmer, it would be nice to come up with a guess ahead of time of what the user is going to add to the computer or the program ahead of time. but this is pretty much impossible. This is where the conditional statements are going to come in because they will make it easier to run the program in the manner that you would like. You can set up some conditions, and the compiler is able to use the conditions, along with the information that the user puts into the computer, in order to set things up as well.

You will find that these kinds of conditional statements are going to work with quite a few of the programs that you want to go through and write through this process. They are pretty simple, and it is possible to add more and more to them as you would need. And there are three main types that we are going to spend our time on, based on what we would like to see happen in the code. With this in mind, we are going to take a look at how to work with the if statement, the if else statement, and the elif statement to see how these are able to work for some of our needs as well.

Decision Control Statement # 1: The If Statement

First, we need to take a look at the if statement. This is the most basic of the three and can give us something to work off when we start to do the other two statements. The if statement is the most basic of these and will only let the program you write proceed forward if the answer provides it with the right answer. If the user puts in an answer, and the program determines that the answer is false based on the conditions that you set, then nothing will happen. If the answer is deemed true based on your set conditions, then the program will display some message or do another task you assigned to it.

You can probably already guess that this will cause some problems with most codes, but it is still important to know how to use these statements. A simple code that you can work with for these conditional statements include:

```
age = int(input("Enter your age:"))
if (age <=18):
print("You are not eligible for voting, try next election!")
print("Program ends")
```

Now, when you work with this kind of conditional statement, there are a number of things that are going to show up with this kind of code. If you have a user who is on your website or using his program, and they state that they are under the age of 18, then the program, as it is written, is going to work just fine, and the message that we have there is going to show up. The user will be able to read that message before the program either ends or goes on to the next part that we have.

We can already see where this is going to cause a few problems along the way. With this one, if the user puts in that their age is over 18, then it is not going to meet the conditions that you place into the compiler. This doesn't mean that their age can't be over 18, but with the if statement, we have not set it up to handle any answers that are above 18.

As we have written out the code right now, nothing is going to happen if the user puts in that their age is above 18. This is because we haven't set it up. Right now, until we change over to the if else statements, later on, the user is just going to end up with a blank screen if they do happen to say that their age is more than 18 when they use this program.

Decision Control Statement # 2: The If Else Statement

The if statements are good to practice within the coding, but there aren't many times in your program where that is going to work. You want to have something come up on the screen when the user puts in their age, regardless of what their age is. If you used the if statement in the example above, your user will end up with a blank screen and no idea what is going on if they say their age is above 18. That doesn't look very professional and won't help you to keep people looking at your program.

A better option to use is the if else statement. These statements will provide an output to the user, no matter what they provide as their input. With the example above, the user may get the previous message if they state their age is 16, but then the code would also have a response if the user says their age is 32. It will respond to any answer that it is given, helping the code to keep moving through the program and ensuring that nothing just stops.

With the voting example that we had above, you can implement the following code to make an if else statement:

```
age = int(input("Enter your age:"))
if (age <=18):
print("You are not eligible for voting, try next election!")
else
print("Congratulations! You are eligible to vote. Check out your local polling station to find out more information!)
print("Program ends")
```

when we are working with this kind of option, we will see that he else statement is added to the thing. This else statement is important because it is going to be able to come into this program and will handle all of the ages that the user can input that are above 18. This way, if you have a user who is older than 18, they will be able to add on this age, and the program is still going to work the way that you would like.

You are also able to go through and add in a few more layers to all of this if you would like. For example, it is also possible for us to go through and divide it up so that we end up with four or five age groups, and each one will end up with a different kind of response in the process as well. And then you would add in the else in order to really catch all of the extras that are left that you did not think about ahead of time.

A good example of how this one is going to work is if you grab the code syntax above and then use it to ask the user what color is their favorite. You could then work with the if statements to help cover up some of the most basic of colors, such as black, orange, green, blue, red, yellow, and purples. If the user picks one of these as the color that they like the most, then the statement that you put with it is going to show up.

The else statement is going to be there because it is impossible to guess what answers the user is going to give all of the time. There are just too many colors out there, and so many of them have different names based on how you would like to use them. You can use the else statement is going to be there to help us catch any of the other colors that the user may choose as their favorite including white or pink or something else similar.

Decision Control Statement # 3: The Elif Statement

You can also look at using the elif statements in your code. The elif statements add on another level, but they are still pretty easy to work with. You can add as many of these into your code as you want, and then we add in an else statement to cover any other decisions that need to be taken care of in your code. Think of the elif statement like the old games where the user could pick from a menu the options that they wanted. This is similar to how the elif statement is going to work.

You can have as few or as many options as you want with the elif statement. You can choose to add in just two or three, or you could expand this out to twenty or more. The fewer options you have, though, the easier it is to write out the code that you want to use. A good example of a program that uses the elif statement is the following:

```
Print("Let's enjoy a Pizza! Ok, let's go inside Pizzahut!")
print("Waiter, Please select Pizza of your choice from the menu")
pizzachoice = int(input("Please enter your choice of Pizza:"))
if pizzachoice == 1:
print('I want to enjoy a pizza napoletana')
elif pizzachoice == 2:
```

```
print('I want to enjoy a pizza rustica')
elif pizzachoice == 3:
print('I want to enjoy a pizza capricciosa')
else:
print("Sorry, I do not want any of the listed pizza's, please
bring a Coca Cola for me.")
```

When we are working with this kind of code, you can see that the user is going to get a kind of menu of choices to show up, and they are able to go through and choose the type of pizza that they want to have in the game. But you are able to go through and change up this syntax so that you have something else showing up in the code that you want to use. If the user in this one does go and push the number 2, then they will end up getting Pizza Rustica as their choice. But if they find that they do not like any of the choices that they are presented with, and they would like to just get a drink in the game, then they could click on that option and get a pop in the process

Of course, this is a simple version of what we are going to see with these elif statements, and it is a great way to ensure that you are able to give your user a set of choices to pick from. In some of the other options, you could allow the user to add in the choices that they want, but when we are working with the elif statement, they are going to either pick out the one that they want that the game has provided, or you will have them go with the default option will be the one that shows up.

This is a good option to work with when you would like to create one of your own games, and you would like to give the user some options to progress the game on. You can also use this for testing someone online, or when you are doing a program that you need to limit the choices that the user will be able to pick out from the code.

These are some of the best conditional statements that you are able to work with when it comes to working with the Python program. You are able to make this be set up in a manner so that it will only able accept the right answer, make it so that the user is going to add in any of the answers that you would like and something will still show up, or you are able to create a kind of menu list in order to help the user pick out something that they would like. No matter which of the conditional statements that you would like to work with, you will find that working with these is going to really help us to get the results that we want in any program that we are creating.

Chapter 7: How to Handle and Raise Your Own Exceptions

We have spent some time looking at a lot of great topics when it comes to working in the Python language. We have taken a look at how to create a few things like conditional statements and some of our own classes as well. We looked at some of the basics that will come with this kind of language and how it can work for our own needs as well. But now it is time for us to go through and really see how we can work with something that is going to be seen as a bit more complex but will ensure that we are able to work on some of the codes that we would like.

In this chapter, we are going to take some time in order to look at a process in Python language is going to be the exceptions. We will look at how these are going to work as we write some of the different codes that are there. As we are doing this, you may notice that the library for Python is going to raise some of these through the compiler on their own. But then there are some times when you will want to raise up your own exceptions to help you see the results that you would like based on the kind of program that we want to write.

As you go through this process, you will find that these various types of situations where these exceptions are going to show up, and often they will look just like the error messages that you may have seen on some of the programs that you have done in the past. If one of these shows up, you should take the time to read through it so that you can learn more about the exceptions and see how they are going to work for your needs.

Now there are already going to be some of these exceptions that are found automatically with the library of Python. If you work on these and try to code with these in there, or if the user goes with one of these and tries to put these into the code as well, then the compiler will recognize that these are not allowed and will bring up the exception against what you are doing.

Then there are times when the program that you are trying to make in particular is going to end up with an exception that you have to be careful about. Your compiler is not going to see this as an issue on their own, but you will be able to take some of the steps that are necessary in order to handle these and to make sure that the compiler is going to raise the exception that you need.

One of the common exceptions that the compiler is able to raise in your computer is when the user tries to divide anything by zero. The compiler is going to see that this is something that should not be done, and it is going to raise up an alert when it sees that this is happening at the time. in addition, if you are working to call one of the functions that you did before, and you misspell it when you want to save it or call it up, then this is going to raise up another exception that we need to work with.

Now, you will find that there are quite a few exceptions that we need to pay attention to when it is time to work in Python. And some of these are going to be found automatically in the library that you will use in Python. It is a good idea for you to take a look at these and learn to recognize so that you are able to use them later. Some of the exceptions that are the most common in the Python language include:

- Finally—this is the action that you will want to use to perform cleanup actions, whether the exceptions occur or not.
- Assert—this condition is going to trigger the exception inside of the code
- Raise—the raise command is going to trigger an exception manually inside of the code.
- Try/except—this is when you want to try out a block of code, and then it is recovered thanks to the exceptions that either you or the Python code raised.

Raising an Exception

You now have an idea of what an exception is and how they are used, it is time to learn how to write one of these exceptions and what to do if one does show up in your own code. If you are writing your own code and you notice that there is an issue that is going to come up, then the compiler will raise an exception. Often the issue is a simple one, but other times they will require some work from you. An example of raising an exception includes the following code:

x = 10

y = 10

result = x/y #trying to divide by zero

print(result)

The output that you are going to get when you try to get the interpreter to go through this code would be:

>>>

Traceback (most recent call last):

File "D: \Python34\tt.py", line 3, in <module>

result = x/y

ZeroDivisionError: division by zero

>>>

When we take a look at one of these examples, you will find that the program will need to bring up one of these exceptions because the user is trying to divide that chosen number by zero. Remember that earlier, we talked about how this is an exception that is important when it comes to Python. If you keep the code written out the way that we have above, then you will find that when the program executes, you could get stopped right here with this error message. The code is going to let the user know that there is a problem. But the message that comes with this one is going to make it really hard for the user to have any idea what they did wrong. We have kind of a long and mangled kind of message that doesn't make a lot of sense unless you have spent some time working in coding.

The good news here is that we are able to make some changes to the code that we have above in order to deal with this. We can change up the message that we see in the exception, so that the user will actually understand what is going on, and can make a difference in what they are adding in as their input at this time.

When we are looking at the example above, you will want to make sure that the message we are working with will give the user some information on why this exception is happening. You want to put in something that is not going to be a string of letters and numbers that are messy, and one that is a bit easier to understand and work with. A good example of how we are able to work with this kind of exception includes:

```
y = 0
result = 0
try:
result = x/y
print(result)
except ZeroDivisionError:
print("You are trying to divide by zero.")
```

Take a look at the two codes above. The one that we just did looks a little bit similar to the one above it, but this one has a message inside. This message is going to show up when the user raises this particular exception. You won't get the string of letters and numbers that don't make sense, and with this one, the user will know exactly what has gone wrong and can fix that error.

How Can I Define My Own Exceptions?

In the previous examples that we have gone through, we had a chance to really work with some of the exceptions that are going to be found automatically in our coding. These are ones that the Python library is already going to recognize on its own and will not need us to go through some of the added parts to provide it to us. But then there are also going to be some times when we are able to write out some codes, and we will want to raise our own exceptions to make this work.

Right now, we have focused our attention on the exceptions that are found automatically in our Python library. These are great to use in a lot of the codes that we want to focus on, but you will find that there are going to be some times when we would like to raise up one of the exceptions that are unique just to the codes that we are writing out on our own. For example, if we would like to work on a code that is going to only let the user pick out certain numbers, you could set up the program so that there is going to be some kind of exception raised if they choose the wrong kinds of numbers.

Working with these kinds of exceptions can show up in many of the codes that we would like to work with, and we will find that you may want to use them in games or some other kind of program. This is a popular option if you would like to just have the user guess three times at the game, or if you want to only give them so many choices to work with.

When we are working with these kinds of exceptions, you will find that you have to do a little bit of extra work because the compiler is not going to be set up to recognize that there is something wrong with the kind of answer that the user is giving to you. Technically, the user in your game should be able to go through and guess as many times as they want before the program moves on. But this can slow down the game and will make it more difficult for them when they don't know the answer and can't get the system to move on in the manner that it should.

These exceptions are going to be unique to your code, and without you writing them into the code as exceptions, the compiler would never recognize them as such. You can add in any kind of exception that you would like, and you can add in a message as well, similar to what we did above. The code that you will use to make this happen looks like the following:

```
class CustomException(Exception):
def_init_(self, value):
self.parameter = value
def_str_(self):
return repr(self.parameter)


try:
raise CustomException("This is a CustomError!")
except CustomException as ex:
print("Caught:", ex.parameter)
```

In this code, you have been successful in setting up your own exceptions, and whenever the user raises one of these exceptions, the message of "Caught: This is a CustomError!" is going to come up on the screen. This is the best way to show your users that you have added in a customer exception into the program, especially if this is just one that you personally created for this part of the code, and not one that the compiler is going to recognize on its own.

Just like we are able to see with the examples that we did at the beginning of this guidebook, we will see that we worked with just a bit of generic wording to show how the exception is going to work. But it is easy enough to go into the coding that we have above and then change it up so that you are going to get a unique message for the code that you are writing, and will ensure that the user is going to get a better explanation of what is going on at the time.

Working with exceptions is a great option when it is time to work with some of the codings that you would like to see within this language. You will find that as you progress through some of the different parts that come with this language, these exceptions are going to show up on a regular basis, and it will be helpful when you try to work with them later on.

There are many times that you will need to work with both types of these exceptions in some of the codes that you would like to work with, whether it is the ones that are found automatically in some of the codes that you are writing, or ones that you would like to raise up a bit in your own code. But knowing how to work with these will ensure that your program is going to work in the manner that you would like.

Chapter 8: Inheritances and How They Can Help You Reuse Code and Save Time

One of the neat things about spending some of your time working with a language that is considered an OOP language is that it allows us to work with a process that is known as an inheritance. These are great for enhancing some of the kids that you would like to write and can save us a lot of time. In fact, they can even allow users to write the code in a nicer and cleaner in the long run. These inheritances are going to be useful because you can take parts of the previous code you already wrote out, and reuse it in a new part. You can then go through and make some of the changes that you would like, keeping certain parts, deleting others, and making something brand new, without affecting the original part of the code as well.

Basically, when you want to work with one of these inheritances, you will find that you are able to take some of your original code, which is going to be known as the base code or the parent code. Then you are able to change up the parts that you would like to create the child code or the derived code. The methods that you will use vary based on what you would like to see happen with some of this code, but overall, it is going to help make your code stronger, and saves a lot of time. Even as someone who is just getting started with the ideas of coding, you will find that this can save time because you can create these codes without having to rewrite all of the parts over and over again. For beginners and more advanced programmers alike, this is always good news.

During the inheritance, you take your original parent code and copy it over to another part of the program. This becomes the child code, one that you can make changes to as you wish, without it affecting the original parent code at all. Sometimes you just need to copy it down once, and other times you will need to do it many times, but the process is the same.

To help make more sense out of these inheritances, how they work, and how they can help to keep your code clean and tidy and save you time, let's take a look at an example of how they look in your code:

```
#Example of inheritance
#base class
class Student(object):
def__init__(self, name, rollno):
self.name = name
self.rollno = rollno
#Graduate class inherits or derived from Student class
class GraduateStudent(Student):
def__init__(self, name, rollno, graduate):
Student__init__(self, name, rollno)
self.graduate = graduate

def DisplayGraduateStudent(self):
print"Student Name:", self.name)
print("Student Rollno:", self.rollno)
print("Study Group:", self.graduate)

#Post Graduate class inherits from Student class
class PostGraduate(Student):
def__init__(self, name, rollno, postgrad):
Student__init__(self, name, rollno)
```

```python
self.postgrad = postgrad

def DisplayPostGraduateStudent(self):
print("Student Name:", self.name)
print("Student Rollno:", self.rollno)
print("Study Group:", self.postgrad)

#instantiate from Graduate and PostGraduate classes
objGradStudent = GraduateStudent("Mainu", 1, "MS-Mathematics")
objPostGradStudent = PostGraduate("Shainu", 2, "MS-CS")
objPostGradStudent.DisplayPostGraduateStudent()
```

When you type this into your interpreter, you are going to get the results:

```
('Student Name:,' 'Mainu')
('Student Rollno:,' 1)
('Student Group:,' 'MSC-Mathematics')
('Student Name:,' 'Shainu')
('Student Rollno:,' 2)
('Student Group:,' 'MSC-CS')
```

Overriding the Base Class

Now that the previous section has allowed us some time to talk about these inheritances and even look at some of the examples that we are going to see when it comes to working with these, it is time to learn how you are able to override one of your base classes or the parent class. There may be some situations where you will work on a new derived class, and then you find that it is best if you are able to override some of the things that were being put into that base class.

This may sound confusing, but basically, it is going to mean that we are able to use this to take a look into the base or parent class, and then change it up a bit to help us work on the new child or derived class that we would like along the way. the child class is going to be able to use all of these new behaviors, coupled with some of the old ones that we saved with the derived class, to get the results that we want in that part of the code.

Of course, this is going to sound more complicated to work with as you start out with all of this, and you may find that you are a bit confused when you would like to use this. But there are times when you would work with this because it will allow us to choose and pick some of the parental features that you want to put inside of this derived class overall. You can also decide which ones you would use later on, and which features are no longer necessary for this part of the class. Overall, this process is important because it allows us to make some of the changes that we want to some of the new classes we make, while always keeping the original parts of the base class that you would like.

The number of times that you would like to work with this, and how much you will be able to override in your code is often going to vary based on what that particular part of the code should be doing. You can keep it simple and work with some of the codings that we did above. Or it is possible to add in more steps and let this turn into something that is a bit more complicated. But no matter how you decide to work with these inheritances, they are useful at saving time, cutting out the clutter, and so much more.

There are many times when you will want to bring out the inheritance when it comes to your Python code. This allows you to take parts of the code from before, and then add in some of the new parts and take away the parts that you no longer want in order to create brand new parts of the code without as much work. This can make it easier to keep the code looking nice, and will save you time and hassle as we go through this process.

Chapter 9: Creating Your Own Loops in Python

The next thing on the list that we need to take some time to look at here is going to be the loops. These can be a lot of fun, and if we learn how to use them in the proper manner, they will help us to take many lines of codes, and cut them down into just a few lines instead. Loops are useful for cleaning up some of the code that we want to work with so that we can ensure a ton is able to show up in the code, without having to go through and write it all out.

For example, if you would like your code to be able to write out a big multiplication table, or list out all of the numbers in order from one to one hundred, you would not want to actually write out each of the individual lines of code to make this happen. This would take forever and look like such a mess, as well. But when you choose the right kind of loop for your needs, you will be able to get all of this done in just a few lines of code instead, and this will save you a lot of o time and hassle.

It is pretty amazing all of the information that we are able to add to a simple loop. We will take a look at a few examples of how these loops work later on, and describe the information that they are supposed to hold onto at the time. And you will be surprised at the amount of information that you will find stored in there. despite how much you are able to store in these, you will find that these are pretty easy to work with.

When the loops are set up in the proper manner, they are going to have the unique ability to tell the compiler how it should continue to read through the same line of code, over and over again, until a certain condition that you put in is going to be met. The manner that it uses to make this happen is going to depend on what kind of project you would like to work with, but you will find that it is going to work well.

For example, if you find that you would like to have the program write out all o the numbers that go from one to one hundred, then you would need to have the condition set so that when the code gets to any number higher than 100, which would be 101, then it will see that the condition is no longer being met and it will stop running the program.

One thing that we need to note at this point is that when we do work with these loops, we have to set the condition before we ever try to run or execute the code that we are working with. If you try to write out a loop that does not have this condition, then the loop has no idea when it should stop, and it will just keep going on and on and on. This effectively freezes up your computer and will mean that you have to stop the whole system to make sure that this works. This is why it is important that you double-check that the condition is there from the beginning to get the best results along the way.

As you work through creating some of the codes that are available in Python, you will find that there is actually more than one type of these loops that you are able to work with along the way. there are a lot of options that you are able to work with, but we are going to spend some time looking at the three options that you are most likely to use in the Python language. These are going to include the while loop, the for loop, and the nested loop. Let's get started with these.

The While Loop

The first type of loop that we are going to work on is the while loop. This loop is one that you can choose for your code when you know the specific number of times you want the code to cycle through that loop. You would use it to finish counting to ten for example. This one will need to have a condition, in the end, to make sure that it stops at the right point and doesn't keep going forever. It is also a good option if you want to ensure that your loop occurs at least one time before it moves on to the next part of the code. A good example of the while loop is the following code:

#calculation of simple interest. Ask the user to input the principal, rate of interest, number of years.

counter = 1
while(counter <= 3):
principal = int(input("Enter the principal amount:"))
numberofyeras = int(input("Enter the number of years:"))
rateofinterest = float(input("Enter the rate of interest:"))
*simpleinterest = principal * numberofyears * rateofinterest/100*
print("Simple interest = %.2f" %simpleinterest)
#increase the counter by 1
counter = counter + 1
print("You have calculated simple interest for 3 time!")

We need to take a moment to look through this kind of example. When this is being executed, you will find that it is going to allow the user to go through and add in any of the information that they would like that pertains to them, The code, when it has this information, is going to compute the interest rates for that based on the numbers that were put in.

For this particular type of code that we did above, we set it up so that the while, which is right at the beginning of the code that we have there, is going to be told that it should do the loop just three times. We can go through and make some changes to this and have it go through it more or fewer times if we would like. But for this one, we are allowed to put in three types of information and see the results, and then the loop will move on to something else in the process as well.

The For Loop

There are many times when we will want to spend some of our time working with the while loop. It can be a good one to spend some of our time on, and it is important for us to use it in some of the situations that we have. With that said, though, there are times when the while loop is just not going to work that well for our needs, and that is when we will want to bring in another type of loop that is going to be known as the for a loop.

In addition to spending some of our time working on the while loop that we discussed above, we may also want to spend some time with them for a loop. When you work with the loop, you will quickly notice that there are some differences, but it is still going to be useful, and it is something that other programmers are going to consider the traditional method for writing out the loops that they want to work with.

This is because there are just so many times when we are able to work with the for loop, and focusing on this and how we can make it work is going to be so important to some of the results that we are going to see along the way. in addition, we will find that we are able to use the loop for most of the situations where the while loop is useful as well. So, learning how to work with this one is often important, and if you are going to learn just one type of loop along the way, then the for loop is going to be the one that you would want to focus your attention on.

When you work with one of the for loops, your user will not go in and provide information to the code, and then the loops start. Rather, with the for loop, Python is set up to go through an iteration in the order that it shows up on the screen. There is no need for input from the user because it just continues through the iteration until the end occurs. An example of a code that shows how a for loop works is the following:

```
# Measure some strings:
words = ['apple,' 'mango,' 'banana,' 'orange']
for w in words:
print(w, len(w))
```

With this one, we can already see that the coding is a lot smaller than the other one, which is going to speed up the process a little bit and will make it slightly easier for you to work with. Take some time to open up the compiler that you are working with and type this one in. This will help us to get some more practice into what we are able to work within this kind of loop, and how it is different from the other two that we are spending our time on here.

The for loop, using the code that we are using above, is going to make sure that all of the words that are in the lines of code above are going to show up on our screen, but they will only show up in the order that you write them out inside of the code. If you do not like this order for some reason, you are not able to change it up when the code is executing along the way, but you can change it when you place them into the code to start with.

You can also go through this and make any changes that you would like to some of the codings that are above. You can add in some more words if you would like, add in some more information, and just make the loop look the way that you want. Just ensure that it is all in the right order before you try to execute it. Once the code is executed, you will not be able to make these changes later on.

The Nested Loop

And the third type of loop that you may want to use in your codes is the nested loop. Any time that you are creating a nested loop, you are taking one of the other loop type sand then placing it inside of another loop. Both of these loops are going to run at the same time, and both will continue until they are complete. There are many situations where you will want to work with a nested loop to help you get the code done. For example, if you want to create a multiplication table, the nested loop can be really nice to get this done. The code that you can use to get the nested loop to create a multiplication table is below:

#write a multiplication table from 1 to 10
For x in xrange(1, 11):
For y in xrange(1, 11):
Print '%d = %d' % (x, y, x*x)

When you got the output of this program, it is going to look similar to this:

$1*1 = 1$

$1*2 = 2$

$1*3 = 3$

$1*4 = 4$

All the way up to $1*10 = 2$

Then it would move on to do the table by twos such as this:

$2*1 = 2$

$2*2 = 4$

And so, on until you end up with $10*10 = 100$ as your final spot in the sequence

You will notice with this one that any time that you would like to take one of the other loops, whether it is two of the for loops, two of the while loops, or one of each, and have them run inside of one another, then the nested loop is going to be one of the best options that you are able to use to make sure that this is going to get done in no time. You are able to combine together the parts that you would like, using the syntax from above, and get some great results in no time.

It may sound like something that is really complicated to work with, but you will find, and be able to see with some of the examples that are above, that it is actually an easy process to work with along the way. it will save up some of the space that you need inside of the code and can be done in just a few lines of code. Take a look back at some of the examples above and imagine how many lines of code it would take if you created one of these multiplication tables without using the loop.

As we explored a bit inside of this chapter, the for loop, the while loop, and also the nested loop are going to be some of the most common types of loops that work well in the Python language and that beginners are able to use when they are ready to write out some of their own codes in this language. You are able to use these codes to get a lot of work done in your program, without having to spend so much time writing out each line of code and hoping that it works the way that you would like. These loops can take potentially hundreds of lines of code and turn it around so that you are able to get it done in just a few, using some of the examples and methods that we talked about in this guidebook already.

Writing loops can make some of the more complicated aspects of writing code in Python easier than ever before. You will find that they are a lot easier to work with compared to some of the other methods that we may have discussed in this guidebook, such as the conditional statements, and you will find that it saves time while keeping the power that you need inside of some of the coding that you are writing along the way.

Chapter 10: The Python Variables

We can't end a discussion on the Python language without spending some time looking at the variables and what these are going to be able to do for some of the codes that we want to write out inside of this language. These variables are going to be easier to look at and work with than we may think in the beginning, but you will find that they do have a lot of power and are going to be so important when it comes to the coding that you will want to do here.

With that in mind, we need to take a look at what these variables are all about and why we need to work with them. To keep it simple, the variables are going to be anything in our code that is able to hold onto some value, especially one that has the potential to change. These are important for our coding because they will ensure that, when the code is running and needs the values, you will be able to pull these values out later and get them to work the way that you would like.

As you go through some of the codings that you plan to do with Python, you will find that these variables are going to be a good thing to learn how to use because they are basically reserving small spots of the memory of your computer. These spots are basically going to remain empty until you have gone through the process of assigning a value to them. But this spot is going to help us to keep the value we want in one place, and ensuring that the value will be called up at the right time.

The variables that you would like to create in this process are going to be found in different locations of the memory of any computer or system that you would like to use. The exact spot in the memory is going to depend on what you would like to see the code do and what kind of value, or values, you would like to assign to the variable as well. This is going to make it easier to find when you want to execute the code.

Depending on the type of data that we are working within this language, you will find that the variable is there to help us talk with the compiler. Basically, these will reserve some of the space that we need in the memory of our computer so that we are able to pull up that information later on and make it work for some of our needs. The compiler will know where that saved information on the computer is and can pull it out when it would like along the way too.

Another thing that we need to keep in mind before we learn how to assign a value over to our variable is that we can often put more than one value to each variable. In some of the first programs that you try to write out, you will most likely just assign one value to the variable that you have. but it is also possible that you will need to put two or more values to the same variable as well. If this is something that your program really needs you to work with, then this is definitely something that you can do. And it really doesn't take all that much work to accomplish. As we go through this chapter, you will see how this is possible and what steps you are able to take to make this work for your needs.

Assigning a Value to the Variable

Now that we have had a bit of time to talk about some of the variables that we want to work with, and some of the ways that they work to help out our programs, we need to look at the actual steps that we are going to take when it is time to assign a value, and sometimes more than one value, to the variable of our choice.

To make sure that the variable is doing what we would like, we need to make sure that the variable has at least one value that is assigned to it. This is an easy step to miss out on if you are hurrying through the program and not paying attention to what you are doing along the way. But if you do miss out on this step, then you are just going through and assigning an empty space in the memory, and nothing is going to show up in the code in the manner that you would like at a later time.

This is why we want to make sure that we are assigning some kind of value to the variable. If you have been able to add in the value over to the variable, and even if you add in more than one value to that chosen variable, then it will be able to pull this up later on, and you will get the code to react in the manner that you want in no time at all.

As you work with variables, you will find that there are actually three options that you can use. Each of them can be useful, and it will depend on the type of code you are working on and the value that you want to assign to that particular variable. The variables that you are able to pick from will include;

· Float: this would include numbers like 3.14 and so on.
· String: this is going to be like a statement where you could write out something like "Thank you for visiting my page!" or another similar phrase.

- Whole number: this would be any of the other numbers that you would use that do not have a decimal point.

When you are working with variables in your code, you need to remember that you don't need to take the time to make a declaration to save up this spot in the memory. This is automatically going to happen once you assign a value over to the variable using the equal sign. If you want to check that this is going to happen, just look to see that you added that equal sign in, and everything is going to work.

Assigning a value over to your variable is pretty easy. Some examples of how you can do this in your code would include the following:

x = 12#this is an example of an integer assignment
pi = 3.14#this is an example of a floating-point assignment
customer name = John Doe#this is an example of a string assignment

As we talked about earlier, though, there is another option that we are able to pull up here, and we need to take a look at how this is going to happen for our needs. This option is that we would take one variable, and assign two, and sometimes, even more, values to that same variable. There are going to be some of the codes that you want to write where you would need to have more than one value attached to the variable. The good news is that the process to get this done is easier to work on than you may think.

To make sure that we are able to get this done, though, we need to work with some of the same kinds of procedures that we did above. Just make sure that when we do this, we have an equal sign that goes to each of the parts that we would like to work with and that they attach the values back to the variable that we would like.

So, a good example of making this work is if we would write out a code that included something like the following a = b = c = 1. This one is going to show the compiler that all of these variables are going to equal one. Or you can write out something like 1 = b = 2 to show that both the values of one and two are going to attach and belong to that variable.

One of the things that we need to remember here when we are working on this kind of coding, to ensure that the variables are going to behave in the manner that we would like to work with, is that the variable has to be assigned over to one of the values for it to work.

The variable on its own is just a spot that is reserved in the memory of our computer. Without a value assigned to it, though, we will find that it is not going to work the way that you would like at all. When you assign a value over to one of the variables that you have, you will find that when the code is executing, and the compiler calls up the variable, the right values are going to show up at the right times.

Chapter 11: Understanding the Operators and Where They Come Into Play

The next thing that we need to take a moment to look at in this guidebook is the idea of the operators. These are going to seem pretty simple to work with, but you will find that they are going to add in a lot of power to what you are doing in the code, and can really make a difference in the results that you are able to handle as well. Some of the different operators that you are able to work within the Python language will include:

The Arithmetic Operators

The first type of operators that we are able to spend some time on is going to be known as the arithmetic operators. If you are looking for something to help you get some more of your coding done, and add or subtract some parts of the code from each other, then it is important for us to learn how to use these operators. Basically, if you need to do any kind of math function in one of your codes, then you would want to work with this kind of operator to get it all done.

You are able to use any of the mathematical functions that you would like under this operator type. And you can add in as many of these as your code will need to get the work done. Just make sure that you work with the order of operations to help get this done and to ensure that it is going to match up in the manner that it should for your needs.

The Comparison Operators

There may be some situations where you are working on your codes, and you find that you need to compare more than one part of the code to another. Or maybe you need to take the input that the user is providing to you, and compare it over to something that you have inside your code, such as some of the conditions. There are many times when we are able to bring out the comparison operators, and learning how to make these work for some of our needs along the way will really help us to get things done and make sure that our conditions are met when the code works the way that we would like.

You will find that these comparison operators are going to be helpful when we want to write some of our codes because it allows us to take at least two, and sometimes more, parts of the code, whether it is the values or the statements, and then compare them with one another. When working on these, you may find that working with a Boolean expression is going to be helpful because it is going to give you an answer that will end up being true or false, which is pretty important when it comes to the comparison operators.

For example, if you are trying to figure out whether two parts of the code are comparable to one another, you would want to figure out if it is true that they are the same, or if it is false that they are not found as comparable, and these are examples of the Boolean expressions that you would like to work with. So, some of the statements will either be the same as one another or not. There are going to be some different operators that you are able to use with this and some of the options that you are able to choose to make this work include:

·   (>=): this one means to check if the left-hand operand is greater than or equal to the value of the one on the right.

- (<=): this one means to check if the value of the left-hand operand is less than or equal to the one on the right.
- (>): this one means to check whether the values of the left side are greater than the value on the right side of the code.
- (<): this one means to check whether the values of the left side are less than the values that are on the right side.
- (!=): this is not equal to the operator.
- (==): this one is equal to the operator.

The Logical Operators

The third type of operator that we are going to spend some time on here is going to be the logical operators. These are not going to show up for us as often as we are used to seeing the comparison, the arithmetic, or the assignment operators, but you will still find that we need to spend some time on these and learn how they are going to work for some of our needs.

When we are talking about some of these logical operators, you will find that these are going to be used when we would like to be able to evaluate the input that our user provides to us, comparing them back to some of the conditions that we are trying to set in the code as well. Along with this idea, there are going to be three types of these kinds of operators that we are able to work with, and these are going to include:

- Or: with this one, the compiler is going to evaluate x, and if it is false, it will then go over and evaluate y. If x ends up being true, the compiler is going to return the evaluation of x.
- And: if x ends up being the one that is false, the compiler is going to evaluate it. If x ends up being true, it will move on and evaluate y.
- Not: if ends up being false, the compiler is going to return True. But if x ends up being true, the program will return false.

The Assignment Operators

Then we are able to work with the assignment operators that are important as well. For the most part, we will find that we can use these operators to help us to assign a value over to the variable that we have. we have already taken some time to look at how these are going to save some space in the memory of our computer, and we need to make sure that we assign the value to the right variable. But we just have to make sure that we use the right symbol to make it happen.

The good news here is that the only assignment operator that we need to work with here is the equal sign. Put this right in between the value and the variable that we are working with to tell the compiler that these two go together inside of the code.

As we can see, there are a lot of great things that we are able to do when it comes to working with these operators. Making sure that they are set up in the right manner and that we use them properly is going to be important. Make sure to review these a bit and learn a bit more about how they are meant to work in order to see how powerful they can be for your needs.

Chapter 12: Working with Regular Expressions

The next topic that we are going to spend some of our time on is known as the regular expressions that are going to show up in the Python library. These expressions are going to be nice to work with, and when you decide it is time to work with these, you are able to continue with the same syntax on that expression, even if you need to go through and combine it with another language along the way.

So, if you are working with another code that would need to work with C#, C++, or Java to get things done, you would be able to use these regular expressions in order to make sure that you stick with Python. This is going to make it easier to add in some of the functionalities that you would like, even when another language needs to be introduced.

Any time that you would like to work with one of these regular expressions, you can head over to the library of Python and then take the expression from the library. You need to take some time to get this going right when you start working on this part of the program. Think about the library options that you would like to work with, import them in the beginning, and then they will be ready for you to go.

You will find that there are a number of options when it comes to the regular expressions that you are able to use in your code writing. Often these are going to show up with some of the statements that we are writing, and we have to make sure that the regular expressions are showing up in the proper manner. to help us make sure that these are going to work well, we need to first get a better understanding of how these expressions are going to work in the first place.

If you use these regular expressions in the wrong manner or you do not pick the right one, then the interpreter is going to have some trouble when it is time to read your commands, and you will not get the results that you want at the end of things. When you are ready to handle some of the work that comes with regular expressions to see what they are all about.

Some of the Basic Patterns to Use

Now that we have had some time to look a bit more at some of the regular expressions that we are able to work with when it is time to handle some of our work in Python, it is time to look at some of the basic patterns that are important in all of this as well. One thing that you are going to see pretty quickly when you are working with these kinds of expressions is that you will not just use them to pick out the fixed characters that you would like to use in the code. It is also possible for us to specify the patterns that could show up in our code. Some of the patterns that we will need in this kind of statement, as well as in other parts of our codes that need these regular expressions are going to include:

1. Ordinary characters. These are characters that will match themselves exactly. Be careful with using some of these because they do have special meanings inside of Python. The characters that you will need to watch out for include [], *, ^, $

2. The period—this is going to match any single except the new line symbol of '\n'

3. 3. \w—this is the lowercase w that is going to match the "word" character. This can be a letter, a digit, or an underbar. Keep in mind that this is the mnemonic and that it is going to match a single word character rather than the whole word.

4. \b—This is the boundary between a non-word and a word

5. \s—this is going to match a single white space character, including the form, form, tab, return, newline, and even space. If you do \S, you are talking about any character that is not a white space.

6. ^ = start, $ = end—these are going to match to the end or the start of your string.

7. \t, \n, \r—these are going to stand for tab, newline, and return

8. \d—this is the decimal digit for all numbers between 0 and 9. Some of the older regex utilities will not support this so be careful when using it

9. \ --this is going to inhibit how special the character is. If you use this if you are uncertain about whether the character has some special meaning or not to ensure that it is treated just like another character.

As we can see here, there are a lot of different options that we are able to focus on when it comes to handling the basic patterns of these regular expressions. Some of these are going to be used more often than some of the others, but it is still important for us to learn how to use these and how to make these work for our needs. When we learn how to work with these, we will find that they are going to be good options to choose when you want to provide the compiler with the right instructions. Without these patterns in place, the compiler is not going to get the right instructions that you would like, and then the code will not behave in the manner that you would like.

How to Do a Query

The next thing that we need to spend just a few moments on in this chapter is the idea of how we can work with some of our regular expressions in order to complete a query for our needs. If we are looking to complete the process of doing a query, perhaps if we are working with Python to help us sort through and work with a database, then we would want to work with the idea of a query with the help of these regular expressions.

One of the things that we are able to do when we bring out these regular expressions is to work with a query. There are actually going to be several different methods that we are able to utilize to help us work on a query that we would like to see when investigating a string in the Python language. There are also a few methods that we are able to use in order to do these queries, and we are going to be able to take a look at these as well.

To help us before we get started on this, though, we need to take a look at the three methods. These are going to include the search, the match, and the findall methods to help us complete any of the queries that we would like. With these in mind, let's dive into each one to learn a bit more about how they work, and what we are able to do with each one to get our goals done.

Using the Search Method

When we are ready to work with our first method, which is the search method, we just need to make sure that we add in the function of search() into the syntax. This is going to be the function where we will be able to match up the right things in any location in the string. There will not be a lot of restrictions when it is time to find these right matches in the strings, as we see with a few of the other methods we will talk about. For example, there are going to be some options that will only allow you to look right at the beginning of the string to see if there is a match or not.

But when we take a look at the search method, you will be able to check whether or not there are matches that occur in the string. If there are no matches in that string, then you won't get a response at all. But if the program can find a match anywhere in the string, then you will get that returned to you. An example of how you would be able to use the search method, and what it would look like in your code is below:

```
import re
string = 'apple, orange, mango, orange'
match = re.search(r'orange', string)
print(match.group(0))
```

Using the Match Method

Along with what we are able to do with the search method, we can take this to the second step of working with the match method. This one is going to help us to look at the coding above in a slightly different manner. with this one, we will use the same code, but switch it out so that we end up with there. match rather than there.search part of the code. The match one though is going to just show us the matches if it is present at the beginning of the string that we are searching through.

So, when we take a look at the example that is above, we will find that the match method is not going to give us any results at all. Because apple is the word that shows up in the string and we are looking for orange, you are not going to get any results out of this at all. If you would like to check out whether the word orange is found in the code at all, then you would need to go back to the search method from before.

Using the Findall Method

And the final command that we need to take a look at when it comes to handling some of these regular expressions in this language is the findall method. This one is going to take a look at the string that we have and will release to us all of the times that a particular word is going to show up. So, if we want to figure out how many times oranges are listed in the code, then the findall method is going to be the one to use.

With the example that we did above in coding, if you did there.findall() method, you will find that you will get the word orange to show up two times because that is how many times it is found in the string. You can do this and get the results no matter how many of those items are found in the string. If we had listed out twenty oranges in the string, then this is how many oranges would show up on your screen with this one.

As we will see here, there are a lot of different options that we are able to work with when it comes to our codes, especially when we work with regular expressions. Each of these methods will make it a lot easier to find some of the information that you need, helps you to find out if there are some more patterns that are in the statements, and can make things easier overall.

Chapter 13: The Files of Python

When you are ready to write out some of the codes that you would like to do inside of the Python language, there may be some situations when you would like to take a lot of the data that you are already working with, and then learn how to store it, how to write it, how to create it and more. All of these are important when it comes to some of the files that we are able to work within this language, but learning how to do this is sometimes a little bit hard to work with.

If you are trying to save some of the coding and the data that you have to make it work for later, then you will find that saving it on a file on a disk, or working with it in the form on an inheritance like we talked about earlier, are two good methods to work with. This chapter though is going to take a look not only at how to handle the saving of files that we would like, but it is also going to help us to handle our files in other methods as well.

Before we dive into that too much though, we have to remember that there are going to be a few choices that we are able to make when it is time to work inside what is known as the file mode in this kind of language. To make this as easy to understand as possible, we can compare it back to how we work with a Windows file in Word. At some point when you are working with these files, you will stop and try to save that document that you are working with. But you can also modify that document and make some of the other changes that you would like.

The files that you are working with inside of Python will work in a manner that is similar. But rather than saving the pages of your document, you are going to take the steps that are necessary in order to save the codes that you are writing out as well. The good news here is that you are able to go through and work with a number of different operations when it comes to our codes. We are able to write out new code on a newly created file, seek out or move a file to the new location that we prefer, create a new file for our needs, and even how to close and save some of the codes that we have. Let's take a look at some of the steps that we are able to take in order to make this work for our needs.

How to Create Your Own Files

The first thing that we are going to explore when it comes to handling these files in Python is how to create a new file. This is a file that is responsible for holding onto a code that you would like to work with. If you would like to create one of your own files, and then write out some codes onto it, you first need to make sure that it is opened up and working in the IDLE.

While were are here though, we also get to choose which mode that we would like to focus on when it is time to write out some of the codes. The neat thing here is that you can choose between three different modes that will help you to go with the one that is going to work out the best for some of your needs. The three most common modes that work with creating your own Python files are going to include mode, append, and write.

Any time that you want to make some changes to the current file that is opened, you can use the (w) or write option because this is often the easiest one to work with. Any time that you are trying to open up a file and then write a new string in that file, you will work with binary files and will need the write()

method. This is going to work well because it ensures that you will get the right characters returned at the end.

The write() function is really easy to use and allows you to make as many changes to the file as you would like. You can add some new information to the file, or you can make some changes to one that you opened up. If you are interested in doing the writing in the code, you can use this example to make things easier:

```
#file handling operations
#writing to a new file hello.txt
f = open('hello.txt', 'w', encoding = 'utf-8')
f.write("Hello Python Developers!")
f.write("Welcome to Python World")
f.flush()
f.close()
```

Now, before we take the time to move on from here, we need to open up the compiler that we have and write out the code. This is going to help us to get some of the practice that we need for later on and will ensure that we really learn how this code is going to work. This code, when it is written out properly, is going to help us to create a file and make sure that the information that is on that file will be in the right directory as needed.

The default directory where we are able to find all of this information and the file is going to be the one that you are currently in. you can go through and switch out the directory that is available and where you would like to store that information, but you will need to make sure that you change that over to be your current directory ahead of time, or you may not be able to find the information that you need later on.

Keep in mind with this one that no matter which directory you are in at the time that you are creating that new file, that is going to be the current directory. That means that you will need to move yourself over on the process in order to make sure that you are in the directory that you would like along the way as well. With the option above though, if you are in the current directory and you open it up, you are going to get the message that is there to show up on the screen.

At this point, you have written out the program, and there may be some times when you need to overwrite the program so that it will get a new statement to show up in a file that was already created. This is something that you can do with Python; you just need to change up the syntax that you are writing out. An example of how to do this includes the following:

#file handling operations
#writing to a new file hello.txt

```
f = open('hello.txt', 'w', encoding = 'utf-8')
f.write("Hello Python Developers!")
f.write("Welcome to Python World")
mylist = ["Apple", "Orange", "Banana"]
#writelines() is used to write multiple lines into the file
f.write(mylist)
f.flush()
f.close()
```

With the example that we just did above, you are able to see that we are really looking at how we are able to make some of the simple changes that are needed in order to see some good coding. Just by adding in a new line, we will be able to make things work the way that we would like. This example would not need to work with this line because it is simply adding in a few more words, but you are able to use this to your advantage in a lot of the codes that you are writing so keep it in mind when you are doing some of your files as well.

Handling the Binary Files

The second thing that we need to spend some time on here is how we are able to focus on some of the binary files that come with this language. This is a bit more complicated and maybe scary to work with, but basically, we are going to save this as an image file instead of the regular file inside of this language. It is actually easier to work with because you are able to take any of the data that you are working with or what to save, and then we can change it to an image or to a sound file, rather than having it be saved on the computer as a text file.

You are able to go through the process of changing out any of the coding text that you write in this language so that it becomes a binary file, regardless of whether it is a picture, sound, or text file to get started with. The thing that we really need to focus on and take into consideration when it comes to this though is that we have to supply the data inside of the object so that we are better able to expose this at a later time. The coding syntax that we are able to use for this one along the way is going to include:

```
# write binary data to a file
# writing the file hello.dat write binary mode
F = open('hello.dat', 'wb')
# writing as byte strings
f.write(b" I am writing data in binary file!/n")
f.write(b" Let's write another list/n")
f.close()
```

As we can see through this one, it is going to help us to make sure that we can take any of the other files that we have in Python, and change it over to a binary file. This helps us to save it a bit easier and will ensure that we are able to keep things organized.

Opening a New File

Now that we have spent some time taking a look at what we would like to see within our coding, such as how to create a new file and how to handle a binary file, it is time for us to move on to the third option that we are going to use when it comes to working with this kind of language. Opening up the file after we have had some time to save it, and you write it out before, then it is time for us to work with opening this up later to do some more work with it as time goes up.

When we take a look at the two examples that we have above, we already spent some time talking about how we are able to write out some words in our file, in one of the files that you created already, and you are able to change up the way that you save the file so that you can make it into a binary function that can come up later on. Now it is time for us to take a look at some of the coding that we are able to use here in order to ensure that we will be able to open up your file later on.

Once you have been able to open up that file, you will find that it is so much easier for you to work with it again and use it. Whether this includes making modifications to the code or messing around and adding some more parts of the code to this, it can all happen when you are ready to open up the file. Some of the coding that we are going to take a look at when it is time to bring out the codes that you would like to work with will include:

 # read binary data to a file
#writing the file hello.dat write append binary mode

with open("hello.dat", 'rb') as f:
data = f.read()
text = data.decode('utf-8'(
print(text)

the output that you would get form putting this into the system would be like the following:

Hello, world!
This is a demo using
This file contains three lines
Hello world
This is a demo using

This file contains three lines.

Seeking a File

And the final thing that we need to take a look at in order to ensure that we are going to be able to take care of ourselves and really make sure that we can find some of the documents that we need inside of this process, it is time to learn how to seek out a file.

Working with these files can be a good thing to learn when we are working in the world of Python coding. We have already taken the time to write out a new file, take a look at how to overwrite some of the data that we see in that file if we need, and we even took a look at how to open up the file. In addition to these, there are some times when we will find that the file is not in the right location, and we will want to make some changes to move that file to a new place.

For example, if you are doing some work on a file, and you find that things are not matching up in the manner that you would like, such as a misspelling of the identifier that we named, or you just find that the file is in the wrong directory, then it may be possible that you need to use the seek function to help you find that file, and maybe move it to the place that you would like.

As we work with this process, you will find that it is easy enough to go through and change up the position where the file is located so that it ends up in the right spot, or at least so that it will be a lot easier for you to find it. We just need to make sure that we are telling the code the right steps so that it knows where to put this.

And that is what we need to know when it comes to working with these files in the Python language. These files are going to help out in many situations when we are working with some of the codes that we would like to handle in this language. Make sure to take some time to try out these changes that you wrote, and so much more. This will help us to make sure that we know how to create a new file, make changes, and then get the files to work in the proper manner that we would like each time.

Chapter 14: Tips and Tricks to Learn More About Python

Now we are at the part of this guidebook where we need to take a look at some of the different tips and tricks that we need to focus on when it is time to write some of our own codes in the Python language. You will find that there are a lot of different parts that come with this kind of language, and learning how to make it work for our needs, and how to really get ahead of the game when we are learning something new, can be a challenge as well.

The tips and tricks that are in this chapter are meant to help you really learn how to work with some of the Python codings in the manner that you would like. This is going to make it so much easier for you to really write out some of the codes that you would like in this language. Some of the different tips and tricks that you can use as a beginner in coding in Python will include:

Do a Little Coding at a Time

The number one thing that we need to concentrate on here is doing just a bit of the coding that we want at a time. it is great news to go through and try to write out hours of code, but when it is time to run all of that code, later on, we will find that it is going to make things a little bit more difficult along the way. Think about how many errors are going to show up, and all of the work that you will need to do to debug things and clean them up if you have to go through pages and pages of codes because you didn't stop and take a break.

It is often best if you just do a little bit of coding at a time. This will allow you a chance to focus on the coding that you would like to do, without having to worry about fixing all of those mistakes. If you just do a small block of coding, and then run it, if there is an error that is found int hat information, you will know exactly where the error is and can fix it in just a few moments rather than spending hours along the was as well.

You should also start out small with some of the codings that you are doing. You do not need to go through and spend hours on coding to get better. This is sometimes a daunting amount of time for someone who is just starting out and can make it so that some people will give up right at the beginning. You should consider just starting off with fifteen to twenty minutes, and then building up from there.

Along with this same idea, we want to make sure that we are taking breaks when they are needed. It is great that you are excited to get started with some of your work in coding and such. But if you jump right in and spend hours a day working on the coding, you are going to get worn out and tired in no time at all. This is not a good way to start out with coding at all and can take some of the fun out of the process as well.

Another issue that comes up here is that it is hard to take a break and stop doing the work when you are struggling with solving a problem. This is often going to be a hard thing to handle. We see that we are in trouble with a problem, and we want to be able to fix it before we give up. But sometimes, when we spend too much time on a problem, and we focus on it too much, we will find that it is going to just make things worse.

Our minds are tired, we forget what we have done in the past already, and it just gets more and more difficult to handle overtime as well. Learning how to just take a break, and walk away from the problem is going to be a big challenge in all of this. And often, once you do take this break, you will find that it is going to be a lot easier for you to really come back with a fresh mind, and without all of the frustration from before, and you can actually solve the issue faster and easier than before.

Do Some of the Practice Options

This guidebook took some time to show us a few of the practice options that are out there along the way for some of the work that you would like to do with your coding. This is a great place to get started to ensure that your code is going to work the way that you would like. In addition to this though, we need to spend some time getting as much practice as possible along the way.

The more times that you can practice the codes that we are learning, the better off you are going to be. Spend some time trying out the code in this guidebook, along with some of the other codes that are out there, and then figure out how you can make some changes and modify some of this stuff to ensure that it is going to work the way that you would like along the way.

You are never going to get better at some of the codings that you would like to do if you don't first take some time to practice. All of the good coders out there are going to have spent quite a bit of time practicing the codes that we want to work with, and you can get better along the way as well.

Print Out Things Along the Way

The more that you are able to go through and print out and execute the code that you are working with, the easier it will be to see what is going on along the way. if one block of code works well, then you will find that it is going to be easier to tell when something is wrong. You will be able to go back and see that something is wrong, and where that thing that was wrong is located, faster than before

Printing off a part of the code is a simple process that will help you to really see what is wrong, and will ensure that you are able to fix mistakes early on. If something brings up an error, or it doesn't work the way that it should, then you are able to go through and fix that part of the code. It is sometimes going to slow down what you are doing in some of the codings, but it is definitely going to make a difference and will help us to fix mistakes and errors quickly, without issues along the way.

Comment Out Your Code

If you find that you are not able to figure out what is wrong with your codes, then it may be a good option for you to comment out some of the code to see what will fix it and what doesn't seem to make a difference. You may find that sometimes commenting out the code that you write will ensure that you are actually able to find some of the mistakes and the errors that are there easier than before.

When you are dealing with some of the options that cause errors, and you are not able to find the issue. Maybe you have tried out a few different things, and it is just not working the way that you would like. When you comment things out, you can continue working on the code, and adding and taking things away, until you figure out the part that seems t be causing you the problem.

If you comment something out and it seems to solve the problem with the code that you are writing, then it is likely that you are going to end up with the solution to the problem. You will then be able to focus on that part of the code, making the necessary changes that you need and fixing it up. This process may be a bit slow and take some time, but it is better than just going in circles on this and will ensure that you will actually find the issue.

Practice Makes Perfect

The more that you are able to practice some of the coding that you are doing along the way, the better your own coding skills are going to get. You do not want to just try the codes in this guidebook once and then never do any work on coding again. This is not going to make you an expert. It may be a good way to get started, but you still have a lot of work to go before you are able to write out some of your own codes as well.

The first step is to go through and make sure that you really know how to work with some of the codes that are in this guidebook. These will help you to learn more about how these are going to work with these codes and gives you some of the basics that you need. Mess around with these a little bit to get the feel for them a bit more, and then figure out whether you can make some changes to ensure your codes work well.

But do not stop right here. You also want to try out new codes and more as you go along. The more practice that you are able to gather up and do each day, the better your coding skills are going to get. You may find that when you spend a bit of time coding and trying out some of the practice tests and games that are available online, that you are going to get this turned into something that is more fun and can help you to enhance your learning overall as well.

Ask for Help When Needed

Sometimes, you are going to need to ask someone else for some help when it is time to work with your coding in the Python language. It would be nice to be able to go through and write out the codes the right way all of the time and not have to ask anyone for help. But coding is complicated, and learning how to make this work for our needs is going to be important along the way, and sometimes that requires us to have someone around who can help us when we get stuck.

One thing to keep in mind while we are going through some of this coding, though, we should not just jump over and ask someone for help the moment that an error sign shows up. It would be nice to get help all that often, but it is not going to help you to learn how to code, and will basically just be the same thing as having someone else do the coding in the first place for you.

Rather than letting that happen, you will need to go through and consider whether you have done all of the troubleshooting that is needed along the way. You can try to find some of the error messages, go through and see how to debug the program, and more. Once you have tried out a few things and you are stuck at what is going to fix the issue, then you will need to consider asking someone to give you some advice and help.

When you do ask for help, try to be as efficient as possible. This will ensure that you will be able to avoid wasting the other person's time and will ensure that you are going to see the results that you would like faster. First, make sure that you let the other person know what you are hoping to get the code to do if it were working in the manner that you wanted. Then explain what seems to be going wrong in that part of the code and what you would like to get some help with.

Also, take some time here to explore what you have already been able to do. This shows the other person that is coming in to help you, that you have at least tried something, and can save time, so they don't go through and try the same things again. Make sure to check out what they are doing and ask questions as they do it. This information can be useful when you try to fix some of the issues in your code on your own later on.

Learn Some Common Error Messages

As a beginner, there are going to be times when your codes are not going to work the way that you would like. It would be nice in a perfect world to write out codes that worked each and every time. It would be nice for us to never have to worry about debugging the program or worry about an error message showing up when we write the codes. But this is not the reality.

Especially when you are first learning how to code and how to make things work in this process, we have to consider that there are going to be some kind of error message that will show up in some of the codes that we are trying to write out along the way. Knowing how to handle these errors and knowing what they mean is going to make a big difference in the results that you would like as well.

You will not be able to learn all of the error messages that you are most likely to need as a beginner. You can research some of these in order to figure out what you most likely need and then get these down so that, when they do show up in your code, you will recognize them and will know what changes you will need to make along the way as well. This will not cover all of the errors, but you will find that having a few of these down will make it a lot easier and can ensure that you will save time compared to just wondering what the error message is about ahead of time.

In addition, we have to consider that sometimes we will still not know what the error message is all about. This is why we may need to still do some research when these error messages come up. You will be able to do a Google search of some of these terms and errors and then see what is going to come up with that. If you are dealing with these errors it is likely that someone else has too. So, it is a good idea to look it up and see what information you are able to find as well.

Don't Be Scared to Try Something New

Yes, coding is going to be difficult to work with sometimes. This is why not everyone is going to come through in order to learn how to work with the coding that you would like. It is important for you to spend some time trying things out, and work with things that are brand new and that you do not know much about. This is the only way that you are able to learn something new and will be able to see the results that we need in coding in order to get that application and program done.

If something seems hard at first, take some time to experiment with it a little bit and learn how you can make it work for your needs. Break it down into smaller pieces so that you are able to work with it a bit more. If you just need to do one part at a time, then you will find that this is going to be a less complicated part, and will help us to get more done.

When you really want to work on a complicated piece of code, and you want to ensure that you are going to be able to get the most done out of your programs and applications, then you have to be willing to take a risk and see some good results as well. It may be hard, and it may be a little bit scary, but you will find that working with this approach is one of the best ways to make sure that you are set to go.

Print Off Some Cheat Sheets

One thing that we need to try out when it is time to work with some of the codings that we want to work with is to work with some cheat sheets. Remembering all of the different codes that we want to use is going to be hard. And some of these will be hard to remember because they are more complicated and harder to work with. These cheat sheets will make it easier for us to take a look over at some of the codes that we are trying to explore and work with, and will ensure that we are able to get some of the results that we want without having to search for them each time that we need them.

The internet is going to have a wealth of information that we are able to use when we would like. But you will find that searching around and trying to find the information that you would like is going to take some time and can be hard for us to handle sometimes. And it takes a lot of time. You will get frustrated and may decide to give up. These cheat sheets are going to be a lifesaver to help you to get things done and make it easier.

There are a lot of ways that you can make these cheat sheets work for your needs. You will find that you are able to go through and write them out if you would like, print them off with some larger print, and more. You have to choose the method that works the best for your needs in order to really see the results and to make your own coding easier overall.

There are a lot of great tips and tricks that we are able to work with when it comes to making sure that our codes will work out great in our Python language. Setting this up so that it works well, and that even some of the more complicated codes are going to work the way that you would like. Make sure to follow these techniques and more to ensure that you are going to see the results that you would like.

Conclusion

Thank you for making it through to the end of *Learn Python Programming*, let's hope it was informative and able to provide you with all of the tools you need to achieve your goals whatever they may be.

The next step is to spend some time taking a look at some of the different parts that we are able to focus on when it is time to work with coding our own applications and more. Many people are worried about getting into coding because they think that it is going to be too difficult for them to get started, and they worry that they will never be able to handle all of the work that is going to come with their coding needs.

And that is part of the beauty that is going to come with using the Python language, and we hope that you are able to see this when it comes with this kind of language and with the examples that are in this guidebook, you will find that you will be able to work with the Python language. This is going to be an easy language for beginners and advanced coders to work with, but you will find that it has a lot of power behind it and will help you to get some of the work done in coding that you would like.

This guidebook has spent some time looking at the benefits of working with the Python language, and all of the different options that you are able to work with when it comes time to work on your program. We spent some time looking at how to write out some of our own conditional statements, our loops, exceptions, inheritances, and so much more. We even spent some time looking more in-depth about the work we can do with OOP languages and the classes that we would like to work with, and this will ensure that we can keep things as organized as possible within the code that we do.

When we are able to put all of these parts together inside of our work of coding, you will find that it is a lot easier to work with some of the codings that we want, even when we are a beginner. You will find that this is easier to accomplish than you think, and we are able to make codes that work with all sorts of projects. And considering that Python is going to work well with a lot of the major companies out there and some of the platforms that they want to use as well, including the Google search engine and some of the functionality of the YouTube site, you can see why this is a language that you are able to learn, and get a lot of use out of as well.

You no longer have to be worried or scared about working with a coding language. While some of the coding languages in the past may have been a bit difficult to work with and would not provide you with the results that you wanted all of the time, you will find that Python is not going to come with this kind of situation at all. You may have even glanced through some of the different parts of this ahead of time and noticed that it is easy enough to read some of these codes, before even starting. Take that as a confidence boost, and see how easy working with this language can be.

There may be a lot of different coding languages that we are able to work with when it comes to focusing on the coding that you would like to accomplish. But Python keeps proving that it is one of the best options out there for us to work with. When you are ready to learn more about coding in Python and all of the neat things that we are able to do with it, make sure to check out this guidebook and take a look at how great it can be.

Finally, if you found this book useful in any way, a review on Amazon is always appreciated!

www.ingramcontent.com/pod-product-compliance
Lightning Source LLC
Chambersburg PA
CBHW071059050326
40690CB00008B/1068